The Gilmore Gun
Echo of Murder

Dennis R. Stilson

Dedication

My heart goes out to those who are left behind
due to death by violent crime.
Perhaps some of the experiences and opinions
expressed in this book will help others better
understand and cope with the ultimate crime
and punishment.

Preface

It seems as though much of my life has been in preparation for writing this book. This project is the sum of many life experiences, study, and conclusions which all add up to being me.

The Gilmore Case was one of the most high profile cases in American history for numerous reasons and certainly one of the most impressionable experiences in my life. While researching and writing this book I have gone through many emotions and experiences.

A brief account of Gary Gilmore's story is told to refresh or educate people that they may understand the unique historical and legal significance of this case. The case that reinstated capital punishment in America should be remembered. The fact that this historically rare and important story is not part of our general educational history books makes a statement of our lack of truth.

My numerous ties with many involved with this account have formed strong memories and opinions which I hope might educate and help others.

Working as a bail bondsman has taught me much of the criminal life and mind. While many years of shooting, hunting and being a firearm dealer have also taught me much about the responsibility of handling guns and the need to protect ourselves.

During my course of learning more about this murder, the weapon and others I developed the hope of turning my rare episode and narrative into something constructive. What better way to learn than from history?

I do enjoy firearms but must say they surely are not for everyone. The fact remains no other gun has been involved in any case that legally affected so many at such a legitimate level. There is only one Gilmore Gun.

Table of Contents

Prologue

In the spring of 1976 Gary Mark Gilmore was released from an Illinois prison on a parole agreement to the care of his relatives in Provo, Utah. He was thirty five years old and had already spent the majority of his life incarcerated. A few months later in July 1976 he robbed and murdered two young men on consecutive days. He was quickly apprehended denying his guilt. But shortly after confessed to his crimes, later stating if he had not been caught he would have killed again. He used the same pistol for both murders which is now known as the Gilmore Gun.

Two weeks prior to his terrible crimes the Supreme Court had reinstated capital punishment after ten years of no executions in all of America.

This tragedy has an inimitable place in American history for multiple reasons. Gilmore refused all appeals for the murders he committed insisting on the death penalty which he received by firing squad within six months of his trial making him the test case to bring back the death penalty.

Articles depicting the Gilmore account covered the world in such magazines as Time, New times, Criminal Mind, Playboy, Rolling Stone, People and many more. There were also the books and movies solidifying both the unique and bizarre aspects of this memorable case.

This was the beginning of the true account of my personal connections and experiences with one of America's highest profile cases, the Gary Mark Gilmore murders. Twenty five years later, the murder weapon came to me and the Gilmore Gun story continued.

Chapter One

One of a Kind

During the 1960-70's while growing up in Utah almost everyone I knew owned guns. We always used firearms and they were a part of our culture. My father, being an avid hunter and hunting guide, taught me to handle and respect guns, just as his father had taught him. Grandpa had an early start; at the age of eleven he was wearing cowboy boots, hat and a six-shooter, herding cattle across the Utah desert on horseback. This lifestyle of cowboy boots and firearms is a family tradition still practiced. While in his boots he learned to shoot, appreciate firearms, and sometimes having to depend on his gun for food and protection.

In our family, the first and foremost thing taught about firearms was safety, and this lesson was fortified with information about the law, maintenance, and common sense.

Young people had to pass a hunter safety course. Upon successful commencement, they then received the coveted "blue card." This card represented the person's triumphant completion and graduation from the firearm training class. Without this card, we were unable to purchase a hunting license.

My first gun, well, almost a gun, was the ever-popular Daisy Air BB gun. This gun could put an eye out if not handled safely. I received mine at the age of eight although I felt certain that I was ready at age seven but settled for dart and cap guns. Some youngsters then progressed to a pellet gun. But my next firearm was a twenty-two caliber Marlin semi-automatic rifle. I had certainly acquired my father's trust to have made such a leap.

The next gun I owned was a single shot twenty gauge shotgun, built by Savage Arms. This weapon could be dismantled into three separate pieces in a matter of seconds, which made it easy to clean, carry, and conceal. Then, at age fifteen, I acquired my first high-powered rifle, a Parker Hale .270-caliber rifle with a Mauser bolt action and a four-power scope. At age sixteen we were allowed to hunt "big game" such as deer and elk. Back then, bear and lion were considered predators and required no license. How times have changed. Whether hunting dove, grouse, pheasant, deer, or elk, we never killed just to kill. We were taught always to use and appreciate the meat taken while hunting. My family was never wealthy people so hunting helped put food on the table.

Many hours were spent with friends and family in the outdoors enjoying friendship and exercise while shooting. If we were target practicing, skeet shooting, or hunting, the time spent was almost always an agreeable outing. Shooting was as much or more a part of our life as any other sport or hobby. The annual deer hunt was an element of the school schedule. We were allowed days off from school to go hunting because that is what everyone did. My sisters and mother were also very capable with guns.

Years later, after living and working coast to coast, while guiding fisherman through the bush in Alaska, I realized that not having a firearm would have been both ludicrous and dangerous. This particular day I lead a group of fisherman to the river. We walked along the muddy trail to the river; I began showing them how and where to catch salmon. After getting them comfortable with their surroundings, I started back to the lodge to get another group of fishermen. While walking on the muddy trail with the fern and grass as high as my head on each side, I glanced down at the footprints left from the prior walk. There, over the top of our footprints, were the tracks of a large grizzly bear. It couldn't have been more than ten minutes before that we had walked this trail. My only comfort was held in my left hand—a sawed-off 12-gauge shotgun loaded alternately with double 00 buckshot then slugs. Granted, being only able to see ten to twenty feet in the bush doesn't give a guy much of a chance against a grizzly; but having that gun gave me comfort and courage.

I didn't realize for years how much opinions about guns differ in America. I simply never considered others' lifestyles. In my early twenties, I met "city people" who were intimidated and fearful of firearms. In their world, guns were primarily used by the police and criminals. I can now better understand how people who didn't grow up with a more rural type of lifestyle might feel. If only they, too, could understand how those of us who respect and enjoy our right to bear arms do not want to give that right away.

I have known very few people who have misused guns and have seen much more good than evil come from the use of firearms. Most everyone in our community took it for granted that each other possessed firearms. So, for the few who contemplated criminal intent, they usually bore in mind that more than likely a gun would be present in the location they were contemplating criminal behavior—whether it was in a vehicle, home, or a place of business. That thought helped to keep order in our community. The police do what they can to protect the public, but they cannot be personal bodyguards. Police are usually called after the crime has taken place. Because it is then too late, we must protect ourselves.

A firearm gives the weak, elderly, or outnumbered a chance to protect themselves, loved ones, and their property. Firearms have played an important role in the founding of freedom in the United States, and in combating worldwide evil.

I have always had an interest in studying, using, and collecting firearms. They are in our homes, businesses, museums, stories, history, and life. The feel of the right weapon and the power of control have always been satisfying feelings, as well as reassuring. Even the smell of freshly fired gunpowder is a comforting smell, like saddle leather or an ocean breeze; distinct, pleasurable, and memorable.

Of course there are those who will abuse anything and everything. But if every item that caused an accident or death was forbidden, knives would be the first tool gone, not to mention automobiles, ladders…you fill in the rest.

Of all the firearms used for good and evil purposes, few have played such an important role in American history as the Gilmore Gun.

The Gilmore Gun, as it now referred to, is the pistol that was used by Gary Mark Gilmore for two murders on July 19 and 20, 1976, in Utah. This pistol is not just a murder weapon. It was the key evidence used to convict a cold blooded murderer and the first person to be executed after the reinstatement of capital punishment in the United States. No other firearm has been involved in a case of such legal magnitude affecting all of America at the highest level. It symbolizes America's struggle with the issue of having a death penalty.

This tragedy brought national and international attention to Utah and to America. Books and movies were written about the crimes. For months, not a day went by without some mention of the progress of this case by the media; the event is still often referred to as a landmark point in time when recalling history and capital punishment.

The first book about this case, written by Norman Mailer, was, *The Executioner's Song*; Mailer subsequently won the Pulitzer Prize for the book. The first movie, by the same title, starred Tommy Lee Jones, who won an Emmy for his portrayal of the killer, Gary Mark Gilmore. Then years later, a book by Gary's younger brother was made into a movie. The book, by Mikal Gilmore, was titled, *Shot in the Heart*. There are sundry documentary videos dealing with the subject.

Gary Gilmore obtained the gun he used in the murders by burglarizing a store owned and operated by a friend of mine's family. Gary committed the burglary only two weeks before the first murder using the same pistol for both murders. Incredibly, after the trial and execution of Gilmore, the murder weapon was returned to the store owner. Often murder weapons are destroyed. Returning the gun to the store owner, as stolen property should be, was still an unusual act by the court. Even when such weapons aren't destroyed, they usually disappear sometimes because law officials keep them though seldom will anyone admit having done so. I'm sure the state of Utah did not completely grasp the monumental importance of this case at the time, in regards to America's return to the capital punishment.

Again there had been no executions in the United States for over ten years. This situation was partly due to a moratorium by the Supreme Court prohibiting capital punishment nationwide for the last five years of this period, beginning in 1968 and ending with Gilmore's death in 1977. There have been only two other years in U.S. history with no executions: 1978 and 1980.

In fact, the death penalty had been announced as being "in effect" again only a few weeks before Gary committed the murders. Someone had to be the test case to complete the difficult process of reinstating capital punishment. Gary's case did just that. He personally made the case historically unique because he refused to pursue any of the lengthy appeals available to him for commuting his own death sentence. At the time, the risk of the use of capital punishment brought great concern to those groups of activists who are opposed to this ultimate punishment. If not for Gary's willingness to accept the death penalty, we will never know when or if capital punishment would have been restored. Thus the murder weapon, the Gilmore Gun, has its place in history with the criminal who helped reinstate the death penalty in the United States.

Of course, in any discussion about the evil use of firearms by anyone including criminals, we must also remember that guns are also primarily used for legitimate purposes, such as Olympic and other types of competition, hunting, war, defense, and arrests. I personally believe guns have served much more good than evil. True, gun-wielding people can do evil; but the gun itself is just an object, a tool.

Other firearms such as guns used by Wild Bill Hickok have also had historical importance. Usually the ones we recall immediately are those that were used in the assassinations of military and political leaders. Other guns that might come to mind are those used in the murders and suicides involving singers, actors, and other famous (and not so famous) individuals. In addition, numerous war stories and relics of armory can be found in many museums recounting famous battles.

Let's examine some other historical incidents during the past century involving firearms in America, and what became of those guns. These were primarily tragedies, as is the case when death or injury is involved in historical events, but these are the ones most remembered.

In one of the most historical events in the history of the United States, President John F. Kennedy was assassinated on November 22, 1963. The rifle that Lee Harvey Oswald supposedly used to shoot the President is a Mannlicher-Carcano M91/38 bolt-action rifle, with a six-round magazine. The firearm shoots a 6.5 x 52-mm bullet. This rifle remains in the National Archives building in College Park, Maryland.

On November 24, 1963, Jack Ruby murdered Lee Harvey Oswald using a Colt Python .38 special revolver. This gun was originally purchased for $62.50 and was sold to someone claiming to be Frank Roman but who was later found to be Anthony Pugliese III. He bought the gun at auction in August 1991 for $220,000. The gun was placed for sale at this auction by Earl Ruby, brother of Jack who gained possession of the gun after a court battle to control his brother's estate.

In the spring of 2008 this revolver was placed on an auction. The seller said he would not consider less than $1,000,000.00 for the gun. Several collectors showed interest with a final bid of $750,000.00.

Rev. Martin Luther King, Jr. was assassinated on April 4, 1968. James Earl Ray was charged and convicted of this murder. The firearm found was a Remington Game Master rifle 30-06. Again, its whereabouts are unknown.

Senator Robert F. Kennedy was assassinated on June 5, 1968. The man accused and convicted of this assassination was Sirhan Sirhan. The gun confiscated was an Iver Johnson eight-shot, .22-caliber revolver. According to the Los Angeles police, who investigated the incident, there are no records as to the whereabouts of the gun.

The former mayor of San Francisco, George Mascone, and his supervisor, Harvey Milk, were assassinated by Dan White on November 27th 1978. The gun used was a Smith & Wesson Chiefs Special model 36, five–shot, .38 special caliber revolver. It was supposedly destroyed, but there are repeated conflicting rumors. It can't be found.

Singer John Lennon was assassinated on December 8, 1980 by Mark David Chapman, who used a Charter Arms .38 caliber "undercover" revolver with a two-inch barrel. I have found no leads as to where this gun might be

President Ronald Reagan was shot by John Hinckley, Jr. during an attempted assassination on March 30, 1981. Hinckley wounded Reagan and two law enforcement officers; these three recovered. He also shot press secretary James Brady in the head; Brady was permanently disabled. Brady and his wife became advocates of gun violence prevention. The Rohm R6-14 revolver used by Hinckley is said to be in a

Washington field office of the F.B.I. I'm guessing we couldn't stop by for a peek at this gun, either.

This particular incident spawned the Brady Handgun Violence Prevention Act; also known as the "Brady Bill." The bill was passed by Congress and signed into law by President Bill Clinton on November 30, 1993.

The law initially required a five-day waiting period for customers purchasing firearms or handguns. It mandated a national criminal background check on purchasers buying handguns from ATF-licensed dealers. So, under the Brady Bill, prior to the sale of a handgun, federally licensed firearms dealers must verify the identity of a customer. The dealers must receive authorization from the background-checking system's database.

But the Brady Bill does not cover private-party sales, or sales by dealers who are not federally approved. The limit to the law is due to the federal government having no authority to restrict intrastate commerce.

Because John Hinckley's gun violence gave rise to the Brady Bill, the Hinckley case is viewed as the second-most-important firearms case historically and legally affecting the United States. The Gilmore case, having reintroduced the death penalty, is considered the first most important.

The Art of Collecting

My life has been spent working both blue and white collar jobs; in my opinion they both have their pros and cons. But through it all, I usually wear one of my many pairs of cowboy boots. After all, my role models wore boots and I like them, so I do the same. And that's not my only collecting passion.

Throughout time we, the human race, have been collectors. We started by collecting clothes, food, tools, and weapons. Now the list is endless. Some people collect cars, art, music, antiques, coins, stamps, or memorabilia. Firearms are my favorite; although I do enjoy collecting friends but they do occasionally change and are very difficult to store safely.

While growing up, I collected coins. After many years of searching for coins and saving them, I decided to take my collection to a coin shop and see what thirty years of work was worth. The results were very disappointing. Later the thought struck me of how nice it would be to pass this collection on to my son. With this thought in mind, I felt much better about the time and money involved in my collection. I now believe the best part of a collection is sharing it with others and passing it on to a loved one. Unless, perhaps, you come across a very rare and valuable item that could help make a better life for you and others.

As we collect the items of our choice, there are certain factors that increase the value of these collectibles. Two factors, for example, would be the age of the item, as in antiques; and the condition, as with any collectible. But the factor that seems to increase interest and value more than any other is recognition; and foremost, documented historical recognition. Did the item belong to someone famous, or was it involved in an historical incident? Was that really George Washington's sword? Did Elvis Presley really own this guitar? Was that flag actually placed on Bunker Hill?

When a collectible has intriguing historical recognition and connection, along with absolute documentation, then the collectible is "the best of the best." There are a limited number of items that are historically significant and, at the same time, are positively documented. These types of collectibles are rare, desirable, and valuable.

It takes time for a historical event to become well known throughout the country or the world. Many times the person involved with the event is deceased, which increases the collectible's value even further because we know there will be no other such items. Collectibles involving famous people and events increase in value over time—more than items without this verifiable type of recognition. Let's look at some good examples of guns that have value due to their historical significance.

October 2003 in California a 44 caliber nickel finished Smith & Wesson gun said to have killed Jesse James sold for $350,000, in spite of less-than-certain documentation. The first documentation of the revolver used was twenty-two years after the incident. There is also another gun owner that claims he owns the gun that killed Jesse James. Furthermore, there is a newspaper article written a month after the killing that describes the gun as a "Colt's .45 and a Smith & Weston." Robert Ford shot Jesse James and is known to have continued selling multiple guns claiming each was the murder weapon. The buyer was not personally at the auction and remains anonymous; so I doubt we'll be admiring this weapon.

In 1998, a revolver used by outlaw Thomas Edward "Black Jack" Ketchum in the 1890s sold for $240,000. Again, who bought it, and where is this train robber's gun?

One of the higher-priced guns sold to date is a Holland and Holland double-barrel rifle that had been owned by President Teddy Roosevelt. No tragedy was involved with this particular weapon. It sold at a Butterfield's auction for $500,000. Certainly it is a high-quality rifle; but being owned by Teddy gives this gun its particular value.

It is difficult to establish a value on a historical firearm, but the best system for evaluating historically attributed firearms that I have found is in a reference article titled "Pieces of History" by Jim Supica. His article was originally published in *The Blue Book of Gun Values*, 17th edition. It is well worth reading. This system rates the credibility of historical firearms and the authenticating documentation by using the following grading system.

According to Supica's system, there are two main factors regarding the worth of the firearm.

1. The first factor is the simple intrinsic value, meaning the blue book value (as if the gun had no story).
2. The second factor is the value of the gun's historical attribution, and that term means the historical ownership or usage.

When assessing an historical gun as a collectible, one combines these two factors along with the credibility of the authenticating documents. Documents are viewed critically, with a five-step rating method:

A = Certain
B = Probable
C = Plausible
D = Questionable
E = Impossible

In the example of the Gilmore Gun, this grading system confirms the weapon as an "A" rated firearm because of the certainty of the documentation. Then, by combining the historical significance and condition, the Gilmore Gun becomes a one-of-a-kind collectible. "A" rated guns are very rare, just as true "mint" or never before fired, guns are rare.

The political and legal attribution of this case in which this firearm was involved makes it like no other. As a collectible, the Gilmore Gun is in a league of its own.

After over thirty years of multiple ties with one of America's highest profile murder cases, I have acquired what is considered a monarch of collectible firearms—and a very unique tale. After reading this story, you decide.

Chapter Two

Gary Gilmore:
From Detention to Murder

Gary Mark Gilmore was born December 4th 1940 in a Texas hospital, but under another name because his parents were on the run. Gary was the second of four sons born to Frank and Bessie Brown Gilmore. Because Frank was never certain that Gary was his son, he often treated Gary like an unwanted stepchild.

Frank Gilmore was said to be both mentally and physically abusive to his wife and children, especially Gary. Frank was a con artist, drinker, and a drifter. He would disappear for weeks at a time, leaving his wife and children. Occasionally, his wife Bessie would leave California where she and her children were living with Frank's mother and return to her parent's home in Provo, Utah, where she was raised. She never knew for certain when or if she would see her husband again, but sooner or later he always came back to her.

As a boy, Gary began showing signs of defiance and disrespect for authority. Despite the occasional beatings administered by his parents, he kept on his course as a rebellious soul. The Gilmore family lived for a while in Oregon later moving to Salt Lake City, Utah. During this time, Gary fell in with a group of bad youths. It was said that even Gary's oldest brother, Frank Jr., wanted nothing to do with some of these boys. Gary shared their bad habits of swearing, stealing, smoking, and causing trouble at a very young age.

Frank Jr. once caught Gary and his friends playing Russian roulette with a revolver. Gary was eleven at the time. At the age of twelve, he began missing school, continued misbehaving, and began drinking alcohol. Although intelligent, he was said to have an IQ of 130, Gary continually resisted authority and the rules.

When Gary decided he wanted something, he did whatever it took to get it now. Not long after the family moved to Salt Lake City and lived in a house that was said to be haunted, they again returned to Portland, Oregon.

Near their home in Portland was a train track that crossed a trestle over a river. Although it was a long way down to the river below the tracks, Gary would stand on the tracks in the center of the bridge and wait for a train to approach. He would wait until the last moment, and then race to the end of the bridge where he would jump off the tracks as the train roared past. His brothers and friends would watch in disbelief.

When Gary did go to school he was constantly causing trouble. He would sleep, show off, or talk badly to the teachers. He dropped out of school at age fourteen. He and a friend hitched their way to Texas and survived a few months by running a poker game. After a short while, they returned to Oregon.

Gary and some others were involved in a car theft ring that got him arrested at the age of fifteen. He was sent to a reform school in Oregon, the MacLaren School for Boys, where he spent one year in detention. It didn't take Gary long to learn how best to survive at that school. He soon earned a reputation as a tough customer.

After his release from detention, he was in and out of jail. In spite of his father's abuse, Frank helped Gary fight charges and helped bail Gary out of jail on a few occasions. Perhaps Frank saw something of himself in Gary.

Soon Gary was convicted of car theft and placed in the Oregon State Correctional Institution. While Gary was incarcerated at this facility, his father died, sending Gary into a wild fit and a suicide attempt in spite of their differences.

At the institution, he challenged the authority of the guards—many of whom were brutal men—even when they would hold him down, kicking and beating him until he was unable to talk or stand. But when able, he would stand again, spitting on the guards while calling them foul names, only to be beaten again.

In an attempt to get his obedience, the institution tried electric shock therapy on him. Finally they drugged him with an anti-psychotic called Prolixin, a tranquilizer that when administered in the quantities he was given made it difficult for him to move and talk. He was released, at age twenty-one.

After his release, Gary committed robbery and assault; he was convicted and sent to Oregon State Penitentiary. While

Gary was incarcerated, his younger brother Gaylen was stabbed and died.

During time in solitary confinement, he began to study literature and to write poetry. He was granted an early release in 1972 and placed in a halfway house in Eugene, Oregon. Although he was offered a scholarship in art at a local college, he threw the opportunity away.

After a month of freedom, he committed armed robbery, was arrested, and sentenced to nine years. His violence in prison escalated and he attempted suicide numerous times.

The warden at the penitentiary had enough of Gilmore and finally transferred Gary to a maximum-security prison in Marion, Illinois. Marion Federal Penitentiary had a reputation as a hard place, with rough guards and strict isolation. Although family members were not allowed to visit inmates at this facility, he did start writing to a cousin in Utah, Brenda Nicol. Three years into his sentence, Gary was paroled on April 9, 1976. His uncle Vern and aunt Ida Damico helped with his release on a work sponsored program. Both of these relatives and their daughters Brenda and Tony believed they could help him. Ida was a sister of Gary's mother, Bessie.

In April, 1976, when Gary Gilmore came to Utah, the state was still a more conservative and safer place to reside than many similarly populated areas. We seldom locked our cars or homes unless we were leaving the area for extended periods of time. Crime was low and people were friendly and trusting, perhaps too much so. At the time, we had the usual problems with youth; alcohol, driving fast, and occasional fighting. But the fights were with fists, not with guns and knives and gangs. Today, Utah suffers from the same problems as the rest of urban America; problems that come with population growth and as people bring their own criminal culture to a place with less crime.

At the time Gary arrived in Utah, the population of Spanish Fork was about ten thousand. Provo, which is the county seat and the largest city in Utah County, was around fifty thousand. Today most cities along the Wasatch front and the rest of the state have tripled in growth.

Utah County, where the Gilmore murders and court saga took place, is about fifty miles from the north to south borders and surrounded by mountains. The valley floor sits at forty-five hundred feet above sea level. The Wasatch mountain range stands on the east of the valley, with barren peaks reaching to over twelve thousand feet.

Utah County borders Salt Lake County at the North border. The two Counties meet at the summit called the point of the mountain from which you descend into Salt Lake Valley and Salt Lake City. Just west of the interstate as you enter Salt Lake County is the Utah State Penitentiary, where both the men's and women's facilities are located. This was the Penitentiary that Gary was taken after his trial and sentencing.

My parents and Gary's Uncle Vern Damico's family were friends. Vern had a colorful, entertaining personality although a little intimidating for my mother's taste. I remember him as a friendly, jovial fellow. He would always ask me to thumb wrestle, but as a boy couldn't compete with his strong working hands. However, it was always fun to try. I liked to visit him with my father at his shoe-repair shop in Provo and remember the wonderful smell of leather. He and my father were both avid archers, belonging to the same archery club. We practiced at the Mt. Timpanogas Archery Range east of Orem and competed in many tournaments together. Being a healthy teenage boy, I remember how Vern's daughters Brenda and Toni caught my eye. They were attractive and always friendly to me.

Gary worked in his Uncle Vern's shoe shop before finding a job at an insulation company in Lindon, Utah about six miles north of Provo.

Gary enjoyed and drank a lot of beer. When he couldn't afford it and even when he could he often stole it. He regularly stopped at Swan's Market in Spanish Fork where I lived, ten miles south of Provo, Utah. This is where I first encountered Gary and was also the store he later burglarized stealing multiple guns, including the murder weapon. The store owners were Gordon and Barbara Swan. The Swan family, including their son Larry was a fellow classmate and friend at school.

Gary Gilmore's girlfriend Nicole Baker Barrett and her two children lived next door to my Uncle's family, the Ainge's, in Spanish Fork, Utah. Gary first met Nicole when he and a fellow worker from the insulation company stopped by a friend's house after work.

Nicole reportedly had a tough childhood with rumors of sexual abuse at a young age and a dysfunctional family life. I have been told she had many short relationships with numerous men. During that time Nicole and Gary would often have dinner at her grandfather's home also in Spanish Fork.

After working a short while at the insulation company, Gary persuaded his boss to help him buy a car at a dealership. When the Ford Mustang he purchased started having problems, Gary tried to trade it for a truck at the same dealership. The owner told him no, unless he had a co-signer. Gary did not accept being told "no" very well; he intended to have that truck one way or another. So Gary burglarized Swan's Market, stealing eleven handguns, hoping to sell them to help buy the truck.

While Gary and Nicole were living in the same neighborhood as my Uncle's family some underage boys would go to Gary to get beer for them. One day, he popped the trunk of his car open and asked some of the boys if they would like to buy a handgun, all guys I've known since childhood. They looked in the trunk and saw the guns he had stolen from Swan's Market. Because the boys were only about thirteen, they were too afraid at the time to take the guns or tell anyone about seeing them.

Gary and Nicole's home was gaining quite a reputation in the neighborhood. More than once he and Nicole left the front door open while fighting or making love on the living room floor.

Over time Nicole became scared of Gary after seeing the violent and abusive side of him. She discovered that he often used the drug Fiorinal for headaches. He also drank frequently, which combined with the drug, caused him to become sexually frustrated making him even more difficult and angry. He made demands and acted impulsively. She decided he had an evil presence within him, in fact one day he told her that he knew Charles Manson, the mastermind behind several horrific murders. She began fearing Gary and what he might do to her. She finally moved with her two children to an apartment in Springville hoping Gilmore would not find her.

Gary frequently hung out at a popular and busy Provo restaurant called JB's. It was a trendy hangout at the time and I seen him there more than once.

A young woman I attended high school with and knew well was working at this restaurant as a waitress. She lived only a few blocks away from me growing up and was very friendly and attractive. Gary had been hanging around enough that she had noticed him and felt uncomfortable with his presence.

One night she finished work and was driving home to where she lived with her parents in Spanish Fork. She noticed a car following her. As she pulled up to her house, the car following her did the same. She hurried to the front door of the house and looked back at the driver of the car and recognized Gary Gilmore from the restaurant. He remained in his car but stared fearlessly at her. At the time she didn't know his name, but after the murders learned who he was. She told me she'll never forget that night.

Gary also frequented a bar in Provo called the Whip, owned by another aunt and uncle of mine the Olson's. A few nights prior to the first murder he entered the lounge, walked to the far end of the bar and ordered a beer. My aunt served him and could tell he wasn't in a good mood. Smitty, a regular customer also sitting at the bar, had already quaffed a few. He asked Gary if he would like to play a game of pool. Gilmore just stared straight ahead replying sternly "no" and nothing else. A few minutes later, Smitty asked him again. Gary no longer responded, continued staring straight ahead and ignoring everyone. My aunt told Smitty to "leave him alone." Gary didn't finish his beer or say another word. After a few minutes he went into the restroom. When he came out of the restroom, he left.

Shortly following that night the police came to the Whip asking if someone fitting his description had been there recently. They asked for permission to search the premises.

With permission granted, they began the search. While in the men's restroom, they found some keys Gary had left in the tank of the toilet. Outside, underneath the garbage dumpster, they found three handguns. These were some of the guns stolen from Swan's Market.

You won't see the Whip in the movie *The Executioner's Song*, and here's why. After the trial, the movie company filming *The Executioner's Song* came to my Uncle while working at the ice plant in Provo. They asked if they could use the bar to film. They declared they would have to maintain complete control of the establishment and that no customers would be allowed in the bar. My uncle asked if the company would compensate him for the loss of sales. They said no, and so did he.

On Monday, July 19, 1976, Gary went to the dealership to buy the truck he believed that he ought to have. He still didn't have a co-signer, but he insisted that he would pay it off in a few weeks. The owner finally agreed, but he warned Gary that he had better make his payments. Gary left in his new truck.

Gary drove around, looking for Nicole. Later that night, he stopped by the home of Nicole's mother. Nicole wasn't there; but her younger sister, April Baker, was home. April asked Gary for a ride to the store. Her mother tried to stop her, but April ignored her mother and left with him.

Around 10:30 p.m. in Orem, a few miles north of Provo, Gary told April that he needed to make a phone call. He parked at a corner and left her in the truck. Gary went around the corner, out of April's sight.

He walked into a gas station, came up to the attendant, Max Jensen, and pulled out the .22 Browning pistol. He told him to empty his pockets, which he did. He then told Max to go into the bathroom and kneel down on the floor. Again he did as he was told. Gary put the gun close to Max's head and said, "This one is for me," and fired. He again placed the gun to his skull and fired, saying, "This one is for Nicole." At least this is what has been told and retold in the Gilmore story but after having a conversation with an officer who assisted in transporting Gary he disagrees. According to this officer Gary pressed the gun against Max's skull meaning to fire one shot but the recoil bouncing the gun from his head then moving forward again in his hand quickly fired a second shot.

Blood rushed quickly across the floor and some onto Gary's pants. He returned to his truck, where April was still waiting. April had no idea of what Gary had just done. They left and went to a drive-in movie. The movie playing was *One Flew Over the Cuckoo's Nest*, about life in a mental institution. How fitting.

They didn't stay long because the movie was upsetting April and she wanted to leave. After departing the movie, they stopped by his Cousin Brenda's home. Brenda said later, "I had a feeling something was wrong."

At about 11:00 p.m., a customer stopped at the station and filled up with fuel. After looking around but not being able to find the attendant, the customer left his business card and money on the counter for the gasoline. A few minutes later, another customer stopped and bought fuel. He also searched for an attendant but he checked the restroom, where he found Max Jensen dead.

Gary and April spent the night at the Holiday Inn hotel. He dropped her off at home the next morning and went on his way. April was under the legal age of eighteen at the time and said she had no physical contact or attraction toward Gary.

The next evening, Gary took his truck to a service station for repairs, complaining to the mechanic that it would not start. As soon as he left the station, the mechanic climbed in the truck and turned the key. The truck started up immediately, with no apparent mechanical problems.

Upon leaving his truck Gary then walked just a few blocks, committing the second robbery and murder. This service station was a popular hangout, being close to Center Street in Provo, which was the main drag for teenagers. That six-block stretch was where we all went to park and drive slowly back and forth, checking each other out.

A frequent visitor to just "hang out" at the same service station was an attractive seventeen-year-old girl. She knew the station owners and workers well. At the time Gary dropped off his truck, the service station visitors included the seventeen-year-old girl, her sister, and a friend. Gary was thirty five years old and asked the attendant Victor Ontevaris, who was working at the time, about getting a date with the young girl. Because the teen was standing nearby, with no hesitation at all she said, "I don't think so." She had seen Gary at the station before and didn't like him. After Gary left, she told her sister and the others present that Gary reminded her of a murderer. She was often correct in her assessments about people and the future, and she certainly figured this one right. Only a few days after that conversation the teen and her sister learned about the murders.

After Gary left the service station, he went to the City Center Motel just a short walk away. This motel was next door to his uncle Vern's shoe shop. He walked into the motel and told the manager, Ben Bushnell, to give him the cash box and lie down on the floor. He did as he was told. Gary shot Ben in the head, took the cash box and left. A witness saw Gary as he was leaving the motel.

Not far down the street, Gary stashed the cash box in some bushes and put the money in his pocket. A little further down the street he tried to stash the pistol into another bush. Holding the pistol by the barrel as he hid it in the bush the trigger caught a branch causing the gun to fire shooting him through the hand.

He hurried to pick up his truck upon reached the service station; he went directly to the restroom to clean off the blood. As he entered he left a blood trail behind him which was seen by the attendants.

Before Gary was out of the restroom, the mechanic and his coworker heard a report on a police scanner that someone had assaulted a clerk and robbed a nearby motel. The attendants remained calm as Gary picked up his truck and left. They surmised from the description in the report that the criminal was Gary and wrote down his license plate number as he sped away.

Gary's Uncle Vern came out of his house, which was next door to the City Center motel and his shoe shop. Vern wanted to see what was going on as people were gathering from all directions. Someone asked Vern if he thought the assailant was Gary. Vern asked, "Why, did you see him?" "No," he was told. "But someone else said they did."

Vern's wife, Ida phoned their daughter Brenda and the police. Gary drove about eight miles to Pleasant Grove and stopped by a friend's house to apply first aid to his hand. While there, Gary called Brenda. He told Brenda that he had been shot trying to stop a robbery and needed help. He told her his location. Brenda then called the police and told them Gary's whereabouts.

Although Brenda tried to stall him on the phone until the police could arrive, Gary left, driving through an unsuspecting police roadblock. The police soon realized it was Gary and he was finally stopped near Nicole's mother's house. Gary gave up without a fight.

Not long ago I met one of the officers that were working the roadblock Gary slipped through, a night he stated he will never forget.

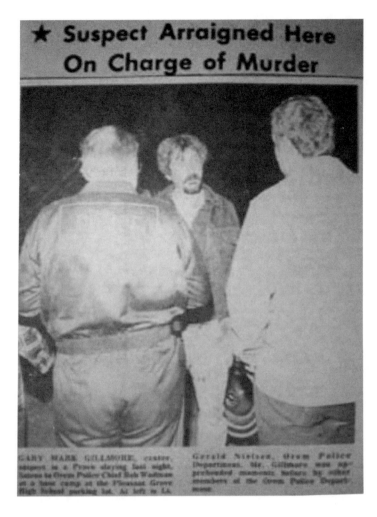

★ **Suspect Arraigned Here On Charge of Murder**

GARY MARK GILLMORE, center, suspect in a Provo slaying last night, listens to Orem Police Chief Bob Wadman at a base camp at the Pleasant Grove High School parking lot. At left is Lt.

Gerald Nielsen, Orem Police Department. Mr. Gillmore was apprehended moments before by other members of the Orem Police Department.

Gary Gilmore arrested as suspect of murder.

Photo from the Daily Herald - Provo, Ut.

Brenda knew that Gary would hate her for turning him in. While speaking with him on the telephone the following day he confronted her about turning him in, she said, "You commit a murder on Monday and again on Tuesday. I wasn't waiting for Wednesday to roll around."

At first, Gary denied the robberies and murders, even though witnesses had seen him leave the motel with the gun ` and the cash box. Some of his stashed bag of guns had been discovered and turned in to the police. Some of the stolen handguns were found at the car lot where he had purchased his Ford Mustang and later traded for his Ford truck. The firearms were wrapped in paper and stashed in an old ice chest.

He finally confessed to Lieutenant Gerald Nielsen, saying that he had killed both men for no reason. He also confirmed that if he had not been caught, that he probably would have continued to kill.

Gilmore told another inmate while in the Utah County jail that he had previously murdered two other men, one while in the Marion, Illinois prison and one prior to that while he was not in prison.

Chapter Three

Gary Faces the Court

The Gilmore case gained worldwide attention, not only because it would be the first execution since 1967, but because of it's many rare aspects - Gilmore's wish to die, the firing of lawyers who appealed against his wishes, the double suicide attempt and his hunger strike.

The jury consisted of nine women and three men.

Gary was assigned two young public defenders, Craig Snyder and Mike Esplin. His preliminary hearing was set for August 3, 1976. Noal T. Wootton was the Utah County Prosecutor and as expected, asked for the death penalty, although no one had been executed in Utah for sixteen years or in the United States for ten years.

Gary Mark Gilmore's trial lasted only two days, beginning on October 5, 1976. FBI lab reports confirming; the murder weapon, a trail of blood, and eyewitnesses, all made a very strong case.

The trial included the questioning of a forensic psychiatrist, Dr. John C. Woods who was employed at the Utah State Hospital in Provo, Utah. Dr. Woods had tested and questioned Gary Gilmore. The judge was Robert Bullock. The following is part of the actual court testimony beginning later in the case. We begin with the questioning of the psychiatrist then proceed with the testimony of Gary Gilmore and the conclusion of the trial.

Q: And what is your education, background, and training which qualifies you to be the director of the forensic psychiatry and the license of a doctor?

A: I attended the University of Wyoming for four years; and pre-med, University of Utah Medical School for four years; received my M.D. degree, served as an intern in internal medicine and pediatrics for one year at the University of Utah affiliated hospitals; and served three years in a residency in psychiatry at the University of Utah Medical Center Department of Psychiatry, part of that training being in forensic psychiatry.

Q: How long have you been licensed as a medical doctor?

A: I would say approximately seven years.

Q: And psychiatry is your specialty. Is that correct?

A: Yes, sir.

Q: How long have you been employed at the Utah State hospital in the capacity in which you now serve?

A: A little more than a year.

Q: When used, the term "forensic psychology," what does that mean?

A: I used the term "forensic psychiatry."

Q: Forensic psychiatry. Excuse me.

A: Forensic psychiatry deals with psychiatry and mental illness as it pertains to the criminal justice system.

Q: In the course of that employment, have you had occasion to do a study, an examination and interview, and testing on Gary Mark Gilmore?

A: Yes, sir.

Q: And that's Mr. Gilmore who is seated next to Mr. Esplin in the courtroom. Is that correct?

A: Yes, sir.

Q: Have you had an opportunity to interview him, test him, participate in group sessions with other members of the staff at the State Hospital, and to analyze him for the purposes of this court proceeding?

A: Yes, sir.

Q: And on the basis of that examination and interview which—well, let me ask you this first, doctor—would you describe briefly for the Jury what that examination and interviewing entailed? What did you do with regard to Mr. Gilmore?

A: The examination entails multiple psychiatric interviews, mental status examination, complete psychological testing, complete neurological testing, electroencephalogram, skull film series, computer actualized tomography scan of the brain, and complete review of all collateral pertinent information.

Q: Did that include background information provided to you, for example, from the State of Oregon and from other sources?

A: Yes, sir.

Q: Now did you and the other—would you relate to the Jury who assisted and participated with you in this combined staffing?

A: Well, there are many people that comprise the forensic unit, and I really couldn't tell you all of the people. Are you interested in all the people, or are you interested in the psychiatrists and the psychologists involved?

A: I would be interested in the psychiatrists and the psychologists who participated with you.

A: Okay. Dr. Van Austin, who is a consultant in forensic psychiatry. Dr. Breck Lebegue, who is a resident in psychiatry and is presently in training at the University of Utah Medical Center and is in training at our facility because we are a branch of the University of Utah Medical Center. Dr. Roger S. Kiger, who is the superintendent of Utah State Hospital. Dr. Robert Howell, who is a consulting forensic psychologist. Dr. Seymour Steed, who is a psychologist on the forensic unit. Dr. Ben Mortensen, who is a psychologist of the forensic unit.

Q: Okay. Now, as a result of your examination and if the factors you indicated, the psychiatric interviews, the background information, the neurological evaluations and other, did you form an opinion as to whether or not Mr. Gilmore was legally sane at either—at the time that he committed the alleged events here or at the present time?

A: Yes, sir.

Q: And what was that opinion, Doctor?

A: We came to the opinion that he was legally sane.

Q: And when you—when you use the term—let me ask you, what is meant by the term "legally sane"? Can you give us a clear definition for that term?

A: The definition of the term "legally sane"?

Q: Sanity in the legal sense.

A: Well, sanity; insanity in the legal sense would mean the presence of a psychosis or a substantial mental illness that would interrupt one's ability to conform his behavior to the law.

Q: And you determined that, I take it, all of those individuals whom you previously discussed, determined that Mr. Gilmore was not legally insane? Is that correct?

A: That is correct.

Q: And you—Well, strike that. Let me ask you this: Does Mr. Gilmore have any evidence of mental illness?

A: He—He has a condition that is a codable mental illness, as mental illnesses are codable under the *Diagnostic and Statistics Manual of the American Psychiatric Association.*

Q: Is that a commonly used publication by psychiatrists to classify types of mental disorders and mental illnesses?

A: It is the publication which all mental illnesses are classified under.

Q: And in that regard you indicate that he does have a codable mental illness. Is that correct?

A: Yes.

49

Q: And would you relate what that codable mental illness is?

A: Personality disorder, antisocial type.

Q: And would you describe briefly what the symptoms of that form of mental illness are?

A: The symptoms of that condition are such things as a long-standing criminal record, for one thing, and the episodes of periodic violence, aggression, and manipulation. A person with this condition usually has a significant figure in their life that tends to help them not face the consequences of their actions. They come from a situation in their early life where there is usually not very much unity or relatedness such as any sort of family unity. They tend to see themselves as not subject to the laws and tend to have very little anxiety. I suppose I could go on and on. Is that—?

Q: Well, if you've touched on the major points.

A: I think I've pretty much touched on the major characteristics.

Q: All right. Did you find any evidence of any other mental illness, such as you mentioned that this was codable in the Diagnostic and Statistical Manual of Mental Disorders? Did you find any other codable mental disorder as a result of your examination?

A: No, I did not.

Q: Did you consider the so-called passive-aggressive type disorder? Is that part of this psychopathic or antisocial behavior?

A: Yes sir, we did consider that. And Mr. Gilmore does have many past regressive features; and this can be classified under the antisocial personality, especially when there are criminal activities involved.

Q: So he does also fit into that particular syndrome. Is that correct?

A: Many aspects of his personality do.

Q: Now, Dr. Woods, in the examination of your—the background and other information which you had access to which you used to formulate your conclusions, did you find any evidence that—well, strike that. I'll start over. Let me show you what I'll ask the clerk to mark as an exhibit. Just a moment. And let me show you this, while the clerk's marking the exhibit.

Dr. Wood, did you find any evidence in this background information, or in any of the information that you used in your evaluation, that the defendant had ever been given any anti-social medication?

A: Yes, sir.

Q: And what medication is that?

A: Prolixin.

Q: And what is Prolixin?

A: Prolixin is a medication that's classified as a major tranquilizer, used for the treatment of psychotic episodes or the treatment of schizophrenia.

Q: And did you determine when Mr. Gilmore was given that medication?

A: Yes, sir. He was given that medication while at the Oregon State Prison.

Q: And approximately what year, do you recall?

A: I'm sorry; I can't recall exactly what year.

Q: Did you also find from your background that Mr. Gilmore had been given any electric or electronic shock treatments?

A: Yes, sir.

Q: Would you explain to the Jury what electric shock treatments are used for in the psychiatric profession?

A: Electric shock treatments are used—well, let's see. That's kind of complicated to answer because various psychiatrists use electric shock for different things.

Q: What do you use it for, Doctor?

A: I do not use it. I can tell you that it is the treatment of choice for one psychiatric syndrome, and that's psychotic depression.

Q: But you would not recommend it for any patient of yours, except if there was some kind of psychotic depression involved? Is that correct?

A: I do not recommend it for any patient of mine.

Q: Regardless of whether it was for psychotic depression or any other form of mental illness, is that correct?

A: That's correct.

Q: But would it be fair to state that some people do use it? Some psychiatrists do use it for psychotic depression?

A: Yes, sir.

Q: Did you determine how many of these electric—am I using the term correctly? Is it electric shock treatment? Is that a fair statement?

A: Yes.

Q: Did you determine how many of these treatments the defendant received?

A: No, sir. The information that I had was not complete in terms of how—the number of the series, and so I did not determine that.

Q: Dr. Woods, let me show you what the clerk has marked Defendant's Exhibit No. 20 and ask if you can identify that just briefly, please.

A: Yes, sir. This is a copy of a progress note and dated November 29, 1974.

Q: Was this part of the information which you received from the State of Oregon and which you evaluated in your analysis of Mr. Gilmore?

A: Yes, sir.

Q: And does that report reflect any statement or evidence of any mental illness on the part of Mr. Gilmore at that time?

A: This report is by a Dr. Wesley Weisert, who states that he is—has given Mr. Gilmore Prolixin intramuscularly, for what he feels is a paranoid psychotic state. He calls it three different things, all of which are compatible.

Q: Let me ask you this, Doctor: During the course of your study and evaluation, did you have any opportunity, or did you—let me ask you this first—what is meant by the term "depersonalization syndrome," or what are the symptoms of that type of neurosis or disorder?

A: The personalization syndrome is a syndrome in which a—there is an intense amount of emotion. The person involved may feel somehow removed from that, depersonalized somehow, that it's somewhat like a movie going on in front of them instead of them being involved in it, or that they are looking at it through a wavy glass, or through water, or through smoke, or something like that; somehow, that they are removed from the incident.

Q: Did you find any evidence of that in Mr. Gilmore's case?

A: Yes, sir, there was.

Q: Now, did you in the course of your study find any evidence or consider any evidence of the defendant's use of drugs or alcohol, specifically alcoholic beverages and the medication known as Fiorinal?

A: As close as we could ascertain, the patient had been drinking beer, the exact amount we could not tell; that he most likely had been taking Fiorinal.

Q: May I interrupt you and ask, what is the medication Fiorinal?

A: It's a—it's pain—a pain medication, for pain.

Q: And what was it used for; or what did you determine, if you did, it was used for in Mr. Gilmore's case?

A: Headaches.

Q: Severe headaches?

A: As he reported them to us, severe.

Q: Okay. Did you—did you find any evidence of any other physical problems? You mentioned the headaches. Were there any other physical problems which Mr. Gilmore complained of?

A: No.

Q: Did you investigate any type of mental—

A: Pardon me. I should—

Q: Excuse me.

A: The examination took place at two times, and the first—when he first came to the hospital, he did have the cast on his wrist.

Q: On his hand?

A: Yes. And I did not treat him for that condition. It was taken care of by another physician. The second time he was at the hospital, he did not have it on his hand.

Q: Now, did you find any evidence of any mental emotional disturbance; specifically, any kind of emotional disturbance on the part of Mr. Gilmore?

A: Any evidence of any emotional disturbance? Could you be more specific?

Q: I hope I can be. Did Mr. Gilmore indicate to you that he was under any kind of emotional or mental stress?

A: Yes, sir.

Q: And what did that relate to?

A: He was under the—he had broken up with his girlfriend, and he had been having difficulties, as he stated it, with headaches. That would be about the extent of it. Along with, I should say, along with the obvious emotional stress of the situation which he was in.

Q: Yes. Now, Doctor, considering all of these factors, considering—let me phrase it in the form of a hypothetical: If you had an individual who was psychopathic personality, would that person have the same capacity to appreciate the wrongfulness of conduct and to conform his activities to the standard of society as a, quote–unquote, "normal person" would have? Considering?

A: He would have the capacity but would most likely not choose to.

Q: And if you added that—if you added to that, at that point, of alcohol, medication such as Fiorinal, would that increase or decrease this person's capacity to appreciate and to understand the wrongfulness of his conduct?

A: It would. Hypothetically, it would impair his judgment and would loosen the controls on a person that already has very poor control of himself.

Q: So what you are saying is that a psychopathic type of personality, or this passive type of personality which you indicated Mr. Gilmore fits into, would have looser controls than a, quote–unquote, "normal person" would have? Is that correct?

A: I think a better word would probably be less control.

Q: Less control?

A: Yes.

Q: And that if you were to add to that, medication and alcohol, that would further loosen those controls, would that be accurate?

A: Hypothetically, yes.

Mr. Snyder: Defendant's Exhibit 20, and at this time.

MR WOOTTON[the prosecuting attorney]: No objection.

THE COURT: It will be received.

Q: (By Mr. Snyder) I neglected to ask just a
couple of—

THE COURT: There's just one thing.

MR. SNYDER: Excuse me.

THE COURT: I want the exhibits for this proceeding separated from the exhibits of the other proceeding, so you can take those others off of that table and put the ones that we are using here now.

Q: (By Mr. Snyder) Dr. Woods, in the course of your conversations and your studies, did the defendant relate to you any childhood experiences which were particularly considered by you in the course of your evaluation, or any peculiar type of experiences which he related?

A: Yes. He related some childhood experiences, and I would say that I would think that some people might think that they were peculiar.

Q: For example, would you give us an example of one of those?

A: This one that comes to mind was the experience of one in which he would walk out on a train trestle and wait for a train to come; and then he'd race to the end of the train trestle to see of he could beat the train before the train would knock him off the train trestle into the gorge below.

56

Q: And did he relate any other specific instances of childhood behavior that one would consider to be unusual?

A: I—some general fantasies about self-mutilation and that sort of thing, which I don't consider to be tremendously unusual; but some people, I'm sure, would.

MR. SNYDER: That's all.

CROSS EXAMINATION OF DR. JOHN C. WOODS BY THE PROSECUTING ATTORNEY, NOALL T. WOOTTON

Q: Dr. Woods, as I understand your testimony, basically what you are saying is that Mr. Gilmore could obey the law, if he wanted to? Is that correct?

A: Yes, sir.

Q: And that when he gets under the influence of alcohol to any degree, he wants to even less, is that correct?

A: Is that hypothetical? I'd have to say, hypothetically, that's yes.

Q: Sir, you prepared and filed in the court on September 2nd, 1976 a summary of your analysis of Mr. Gilmore in connection with Dr. Van Austin and Dr. Breck—

A: Lebegue.

Q: Lebegue?

A: Yes.

Q: Is that correct? Do you recall that before?

A: Yes, sir.

Q: Was it an accurate summary, in fact, of your analysis of this man?

A: Yes, sir.

Q: Part of that report indicated that—I'm reading from it: "We do not find him to be psychotic or 'insane.' We can find no evidence of organic neurological disease, disturbed thought processes, altered perception of reality, inappropriate affect or mood, or lack of insight. His personality structure is dominated by impulsiveness, rationalizations of his behavior, low frustration tolerance, callousness, and immediate need for gratification." Is that still your opinion?

A: Yes, sir.

Q: You go on to say in another portion of the report: "...we do not feel that he was mentally ill at the time of the alleged acts. We find that at the time of the alleged act he had the capacity to appreciate the wrongfulness of the act and to conform his behavior to the requirements of the law. We have carefully considered his voluntary use of alcohol, medication (Fiorinal) at the time of the act and do not feel that this altered his responsibility." Is that still your opinion?

A: Yes, sir.

Q: You go on to say, "We have likewise considered his alleged partial amnesia for the alleged event on 7/20/76 and feel that it is too circumscript and convenient to be valid." Is that still your opinion?

A: Yes, sir.

MR. WOOTTON: Thank you. That's all.

REDIRECT EXAMINATION OF DR. JOHN C. WOODS, BY BEN SNYDER, ATTORNEY FOR GARY GILMORE

THE CLERK: Be seated in the witness chair, please.

Q: Dr. Woods, was this report made in the connection of your determining whether or not Gilmore was insane in the legal sense?

A: Yes, sir.

Q: This report?
A: Yes, sir. It was.
MR. SNYDER: That's all.
THE COURT: All right. Doctor, you may step down.
MR. SNYDER: Call the defendant, Gary Gilmore.
Step forward, raise your right hand and be sworn.

Mr. Gilmore, having been called as witness, being first sworn, testifies as follows:

DIRECT EXAMINATION OF GARY MARK GILMORE, BY BEN SNYDER, ATTORNEY FOR GARY GILMORE

THE CLERK: Be seated in the witness chair, please.
Q: (Mr. Snyder) Would you state your name, please?
A: Gary Gilmore.
Q: You are the defendant in the action which is presently before the Court, is that correct?
A: Yes.
Q: Mr. Gilmore, calling your attention to the day of July 20, 1976, do you recall that particular day?
A: Yes, I do.
Q: Could you state for the Court, beginning with your activities, say from noon on, what your activities were during that day, up to about ten o'clock in the evening?
THE COURT: Mr. Snyder?
MR. SNYDER: Yes, sir?
THE COURT: I think I ought to advise the defendant at this time that he may be subject to cross-examination as to the matters that he testifies to. However, I will not permit

cross-examination beyond the subject matter of his direct testimony.

MR. SNYDER: I have advised the defendant of that previously, Your Honor; and I think the defendant is aware of that.

THE COURT: All right. Go ahead.

Q: (By Mr. Snyder) Do you understand that, Mr. Gilmore?

A: Yes, I do. Thank you.

Q: Calling your attention, then, to the day of July 20, 1976 of from, say, at noon, the hour of noon, until approximately ten o'clock in the evening. Do you recall your activities briefly on that day, and could you relate them to the jury?

A: I recall them briefly. I only recall some things.

Q: Would you relate them, please, to the jury, the ones you do recall?

A: I got off work about 1:30 to go look for an apartment.

Q: Where were you working at the time, Mr. Gilmore?

A: At Ideal Insulation in Lindon.

Q: Go on. I'm sorry to interrupt.

A: And I didn't look for an apartment. I went over to my aunt's house and took a shower, and I went and bought a pair of pants, and I changed clothes, and I drank a little beer and drove out to Spanish Fork and talked with a neighbor. I had been living in Spanish Fork. And I drove around for a bit. I don't remember exactly everything I did every minute.

Q: Okay. Calling your attention to the evening—well, let me ask you this: During the course of that particular day, did you have an occasion to drink any alcoholic beverage?

A: Yeah. I drank some beer.

Q: Approximately how much beer did you drink, if you recall?

A: I don't know. Maybe a half a case.

Q: How many cans or bottles are in a case, if you know?

A: There's twenty-four.

Q: So you think you had about twelve cans of beer?

A: Yeah, I would say about twelve.

Q: Were you taking any medication, Mr. Gilmore?

A: Yes. It's a mild pain medication.

Q: Had you taken that medication on previous occasions for headache pain?

A: Yes.

Q: And let me take you now till up to the hour of approximately 10:30 in the evening. Did you have occasion to park your truck at a service station, which we have heard previous testimony about, on the corner of University and Third South, I believe it is, in the city of Provo?

A: Yes, I did.

Q: What did you take your truck there for?

A: Well, it wouldn't start every time. I didn't know what was the matter with it.

Q: Did you—were you acquainted with the people who operated that service station?

A: Yes, I was acquainted with them.

Q: Had they previously done work for you on your vehicle?

A: Yes.

Q: And you were acquainted, then, with Mr. Ontiveros. Is that correct?

A: Right.

Q: And after you left your truck at the service station that evening, where did you go?

A: Well, I walked down the street to an apartment house to see a girl.

Q: And did you, in fact, see the girl?

A: No, she wasn't there.

Q: What did you do after you got through doing that?

A: I went back down the street. I guess they weren't home.

Q: Where do your uncle and aunt reside?

A: 130 West Third South.

Q: Is that in the city of Provo?

A: Yes.

Q: And they—nobody answered, is that correct, or nobody was at their residence?

A: No, I guess not. I didn't see them. No.

Q: What did you do after you did that?

A: I went over to the City Center Motel.

Q: And would you describe what, if anything, occurred at the City Center Motel?

A: Well, I told the guy I would like to have a room for the night.

Q: Did you subsequently get a room?

A: No.

Q: Mr. Gilmore, did you kill Mr. Bushnell?

A: Yes, I guess I did.

Q: Did you intend to kill Mr. Bushnell at the time that you went to the City Center Motel?

A: No.

Q: Why did you kill Bennie Bushnell?

A: I don't know.

Q: Could you give the Jury any explanation as to why you did it? Can you tell the Jury how you felt at the time you did it?

MR. WOOTTON: Well, we object. Let's have one question at a time.

Q: (By Mr. Snyder) Let me ask you this, Mr. Gilmore: Can you tell the Jury how you felt at the time you—at the time these events were occurring?

A: I don't know. I can tell you how—I can—I felt—just how I felt, I don't know for sure.

Q: Go ahead.

A: Well, I felt like there was no way that what happened could have been avoided; that there was no other choice or chance for Mr. Bushnell. It was just something that, you know, couldn't be stopped.

Q: Do you feel like you had control of yourself or your actions?

A: No, I don't.

Q: Do you feel like—well, let me ask you this: Do you know why you killed Bennie Bushnell?

A: No.

Q: Did you need the money?

A: No.

Q: How did you feel at the time? You described that you felt like you couldn't control yourself, but how—can you describe any other circumstances—anything else that you felt?

A: I felt like I was watching a movie or, you know, somebody else was perhaps doing this and I was watching them doing it.

Q: Do you feel like you were seeing yourself do it?

A: Not quite to the extent where I would be off seeing myself do something, no.

Q: Do you feel like you were seeing someone else do it?

A: A little, I guess. I don't really know. I can't recall that clearly. There were spots that night that I don't recall at all, some of it is sharper than others, and some of it is totally blank.

Q: Did you have any emotional or physical problems on July 20, 1972—or 1976? Excuse me.

A: I didn't have any physical problems. I was pretty pushed out of shape on something.

Q: About what?

A: A personal matter.

Q: Did it involve a friend of yours?

A: Yes.

Q: Had you a disagreement with that friend?

A: Yes, sir.

Q: Now, did you explain and relate these circumstances to Dr. Woods and the other doctors who interviewed you and talked to you at the State Hospital and elsewhere?

A: Summarily. I wasn't able to talk to them.

Q: Why weren't you able to talk to them?

A: Well, they wouldn't interview me privately. They wouldn't give me the privacy of a private interview, and they had in-patients sitting there. For security reasons, they claimed. But they were sitting there monitoring the interviewing. Some people may have been able to accept this, but I had real strong feelings against it. So I just was cursory in my answers and, you know, in the way I related to the doctors at the hospital, for that and other reasons.

Q: Have you had prior experiences with psychiatrists and psychologists in prison, which caused you to have this adverse reaction?

A: Yes.

Q: Could you briefly relate what those experiences have been?

A: Well, I was chained hand and foot flat on my back two weeks to a bed. I wasn't allowed to get up and use the bedpan. And by—at the orders of a psychiatrist. I mean, I will never understand how and why, you know, it happened.

Q: Have you been given any medication by a psychiatrist to treat any psychotic or other behavior that you have exhibited?

A: I was put on a drug called Prolixin for four months.

Q: What effect did that drug have on you?

A: Totally paralyzed me.

Q: Were you able to move?

A: I had to get help a lot of the times to stand up.

Q: How long were you given that drug?

A: For four months.

Q: Have you ever received any electric shock treatments?

A: Yes, sir.

Q: Why were you given those?

A: Well, I got drunk. I was in the joint and I got drunk. I tore up a cell. And they put me in the hole—the psychiatrist they had working at the prison then. It's a secure-all for everything. And he violently gave me electric shock therapy.

Q: How many of these treatments did you receive?

A: They told me six. It's pretty hard to remember anything after even one of them.

Q: Mr. Gilmore, do you recall relaying to Dr. Woods, and the other people who talked with you at the State Hospital, a childhood experience such as the one Dr. Woods described; standing in the middle of a railroad track with a train coming toward you, and then you run across a trestle to beat the train?

A: Yes. I didn't tell him that particular incident. Well, it was a series of incidents. I didn't tell him that to be traumatic or anything. I was trying to give him a comparison to the urge and the impulse that I felt on the night of July 20th. I sometimes feel I have to do things and seems like there's no other chance or choice. I—so I was using that for comparative purposes.

Q: I see. And is that similar to the way that you felt on the night of July 20, 1976?

A: Similar. Very similar. Yeah, it would be. Sometimes I would feel an urge to do something, and I would try to put it off; and the urge would become stronger until it was irresistible; and that's the way I felt on the night of July 20th.

Q: Felt like you had no control over what you did?

A: Yes.

MR. SNYDER: May I have a moment, Your Honor? Your witness.

CROSS EXAMINATION OF GARY MARK GILMORE, BY NOALL T WOOTTON, PROSECUTING ATTORNEY

Q: How did you kill him?

A: Shot him.

Q: Tell me about it. Tell me what you did.

A: I shot him.

Q: Did you lay him down on the floor?

A: Not with my own hands, no.

Q: Did you tell him to get down on the floor?

A: Yes, I did.

Q: Face down?

A: No, I don't know if I went into all that much detail, Wootton.

Q: Did he lay down, face down?

A: He laid down on the floor.

Q: Did you put the gun up against his head?

A: I suppose I did.

Q: Did you pull the trigger?

A: Yeah.

Q: Then what did you do?

A: I left.

Q: Did you take the cash box with you?

A: I don't recall taking the cash box with me.

Q: But you saw it in the courtroom, didn't you?

A: Yes, I saw what you said was the cash box sitting there.

Q: You don't ever remember seeing that before?

A: No.

Q: Did you take his money?

A: I don't recall that either, I said.

Q: Do you remember taking any money?

A: I don't recall that either.

Q: Do you remember taking any money?

A: I don't recall that either, I said.

Q: Do you remember having some money on you when you were arrested later that night?

A: I always had money on me.

Q: How much did you have on you?

A: I don't know.

Q: You don't have any idea?

A: I don't have a bank account. I always just carried my money in my pocket.

Q: You don't know where it came from?

A: Well, I got paid Friday. That wasn't too long before that.

Q: You said you were pushed out of shape that night over a personal matter. Why don't you tell us about that?

A: I'd rather not.

Q: Are you refusing?

A: Right.

Q: Even if the Court tells you that you have to, you won't?

A: Right.

Q: Did that make you feel like you wanted to kill something?

A: I'd rather not answer that.

Q: How long had you had the gun with you?

A: Just a matter of hours, I guess. I don't recall exactly when I picked it up.

Q: Did you have it when you took your truck to the service station?

A: I had it in my belt.

Q: Did you have any idea of what you were going to do with it?

A: No, not a conscious idea. I hadn't made any plans, or stuff, about doing anything with the gun. I just had it with me at that point.

Q: Why?

A: I don't know. I just did.

MR. WOOTTON: That's all.

MR. SNYDER [Gary's lawyer]: Nothing further.

THE COURT: You may step down, Mr. Gilmore. Take your seat at the counsel table, please.

MR. SNYDER: We rest, Your Honor.

MR. WOOTTON: Nothing further.

THE COURT: At this time, as the statute permits, I'll permit the State's attorney, both attorneys for the defendant, and the defendant, to make any argument they care to that is relevant to the sentence to be imposed.

MR. WOOTTON: Mr. Snyder, Mr. Esplin, Your Honor, Ladies and Gentleman: From everything that I have heard, everything that I know about this case, I can only arrive at two conclusions. First of all, Bennie Bushnell did not deserve to die. He didn't do anything to cause this or to stimulate the defendant into doing what he did. Bennie Bushnell was a helpless victim. He's a victim not only of the defendant, but he's a victim of someone there in letting the defendant out of prison. According to the records as best as I can observe them, in listening to the witnesses, Gary Gilmore spent the better part of the last twelve years in prison. He's only been outside since April of 1976, and within three months, he killed someone. He says he killed someone else, at least he told one girl that. Now there was nothing, apparently, that Bennie could do to defend himself against this situation. It's hard to comprehend, really; and it's hard for me to get across to you the real grief that this kind of behavior on the part of Gary Gilmore has caused to Bennie's wife and his children.

MR. SNYDER: Your Honor, I object to the introduction of that kind of prejudicial statement in the argument by the counsel. I think that we need to make that comment on the record, because I don't think that's a matter that is properly before the Jury in this case, and I'd reserve a motion in that regard at this time.

THE COURT: All right. I'll reserve your—a ruling on your motion. I'll ask Mr. Wootton to omit any further reference to that matter.

MR. WOOTTON: What the defendant did, in my judgment, alone, apart from any other prior history, is sufficient to justify the death penalty in this case. But let's look at the kind of man the defendant is. For the last twelve years he's been in prison. He's been out since April of 1976.

All rehabilitation attempts apparently have been a total, dismal, complete failure. Now, if you can't rehabilitate somebody in twelve years, can you expect to ever rehabilitate him at all? He tells you he killed Bennie. He tells you he doesn't know why. He tells you how. He told him to lay down on the floor and he put a gun to his head and pulled the trigger. That's pretty cold-blooded. Now he's been convicted on two prior occasions of robbery. One, as I recall, was specifically an armed robbery; the other I don't know whether it was or not. But he served time for those. And he's learned something because of that time. Do you know what it is? He's going to kill his victims. Now, that's smart. If you are going to make your living as a robber, that just makes sense, because a dead victim is not going to identify you. He'd have gotten away with this, most likely free and clear, except for some dumb, bad luck. He accidentally shot himself. Those things happen, I suppose, when you have been drinking a little bit and fooling around with guns. He accidentally shot himself. As a result he tipped off, apparently, a pretty sharp service station attendant, who, without the presence of mind of calling the police, would have let Gary go, and most likely wouldn't have caught him. Sure, Pete Arroyo saw him, but he didn't know who he was. We wouldn't have had the faintest idea where to go except he accidentally shot himself, so he got caught. But the only other witness to that incident was dead. That's what he learned from being in prison.

Now, he's also got a history of escape—three times from some sort of reform school and once from the Oregon State Penitentiary. His problems in the Oregon State Penitentiary were such that they had to transfer him to a federal penitentiary, from where he was subsequently released. Now what does that tell you? If you people tell us to lock Gary

Gilmore up for life, whatever that means, we can't guarantee it. We cannot guarantee that he won't escape again. He's got a history of it. He's apparently pretty good at it. If he's ever free again, nobody who ever comes in contact with him is going to be safe if they happen to have something that he happens to want.

Now, he's got a history of violence in the prison. Even the other prisoners, if you tell us to send him to prison, cannot be guaranteed safety from his behavior. What, then, is the point at this time of allowing him to continue to live? Rehabilitation is hopeless. He's a danger if he escapes. He's a danger if he doesn't. Obviously nothing can be done to save this man at this point. He's an extremely high escape risk. He's an extreme danger to anybody. Without even considering all these factors, however, I submit to you this: For what he did to Bennie Bushnell and the position that he's put Bennie's wife in, he has forfeited his right to live any longer and he should be executed, and I recommend that to you.

THE COURT: Mr. Snyder? Mr. Esplin?

MR. ESPLIN: Your Honor, Mr. Snyder will argue
for the—

THE COURT: All right.

MR. SNYDER: I suppose that nobody feels worse about what happened to Ben Bushnell and to his family than I do. This has been a very difficult case for me personally to even try. I think that it puts the Jury in a position that I would not want to be in, because in spite of the fact that this type of crime was committed in this particular case, what we are dealing with here is human life. Mr. Gilmore is a person, too; and although Mr. Gilmore has a history of prior conduct which hopefully we can all learn something from and which hopefully none of us will have to come in contact with again, he is a person and, in my opinion, he has a right to his life. I don't think there's anything more personal to any individual than his right to live. And you are in the position at this point where you have to decide whether to take that life from Gary Gilmore or whether to let him live. I don't excuse what Mr. Gilmore did, I don't even pretend to try to explain it; but I think he does have the right to live, and I would ask that you give him that opportunity.

I think the sum of what Mr. Wootton says is well taken. I think that Mr. Gilmore's history is certainly something that he's not proud of. I don't think any of us are. But I think that the evidence that we heard in the form of statements from the probation agent and from others was not evidence that he's a person that's likely to escape. He did escape from reform school when he was age—before he was eighteen-years-old. Apparently he did walk away from the Oregon State Prison when he was out on school release; but he's not the type of person, I don't think, and in my opinion, that is likely to even try that type of thing. And I'd point out to you a couple of specific instances which you are as much aware of as I am. I'm not sure that this defendant's behavior is anything more than the mental illness, the type of mental problem that Dr. Woods described. He indicated—and the statute indicates to you, that you can consider and you can take into consideration any mental disease or impairment, particularly if it's compounded by intoxication or the influence of drugs. That's in the Jury instructions that you'll be allowed to take into the courtroom with you. I don't think—the reason I don't think that Mr. Gilmore is—his behavior in normal circumstances is something that he, absent these other factors, is something that he would not be able to cope with and control is simply for two reasons:

Number one—there was one person in this case that he could have shot and killed that he didn't. If he had been that bloodthirsty, able to cope, or so in control of his actions—the first person I'd have shot after I had committed such a blood thirsty act was Pete Arroyo. You remember Mr. Arroyo said, "He looked right at me. The only thing that was separating us was a windowpane and glass. He looked right into my eyes." But he didn't shoot Pete Arroyo. He didn't make any move toward him. I think that's the type of demonstration, the type of activity that indicates that Mr. Gilmore does have something that maybe he can't cope with; but it's not something that we ought to take his life for.

The other example that I point out to you is an example that occurred right here in the courtroom. And it's just a little thing, it doesn't really mean very much. But you remember when we were looking at the exhibits, when Mr. Wootton had had the F.B.I. agent on the stand and he was looking at the gun, and the bullets, and the casings, and so forth, he took the gun and the exhibit and he placed it on the desk here next to Mr. Esplin. Mr. Esplin took the gun out of the plastic, and really, without even thinking much about it, he set it right in front of Mr. Gilmore for me to look at seated next to him. Mr. Gilmore didn't do anything with that gun. He didn't make any kind of an attempt to go for it, or do anything of that nature. I suppose it would have been a very foolish thing for him to do; but I point that out to you that just because I think that in a normal situation when he is not compelled by the type of psychopathies, even psychotic behavior that is referred to in this letter from Dr. Weisert, that Mr. Gilmore is the type of person that needs more treatment more than he needs to be killed. He needs, I think, to be punished for what he does, and the law provides for that by a term of life imprisonment. And I don't think that Mr. Wootton's fears about rehabilitation or that if he ever gets out again, that type of thing, are founded. Mr. Gilmore's thirty-six years old.

MR. GILMORE: Thirty-five.

MR. SNYDER: Thirty-five years old. He is going to be incarcerated, if you will, for life. That's a long, long time. And though I suppose at some point in the future, after many years, he may be eligible for parole; but that's a long, long ways away.

But I ask you to take a look at, for example, Dr. Weisert's note, to consider the testimony of Dr. Woods. You remember that Dr. Woods did indicate that if Mr. Gilmore had been psychotic, if he had the type of behavior that's described that constitutes legal insanity, that could have been raised on his behalf in this case. Dr. Woods doesn't think he did at the time, and he doesn't think he does now, but there is evidence from Dr. Weisert that he may have had that type of behavior in the past. And if that were the case in this case, I think he deserves the same opportunity, really, that Bennie Bushnell should have had. And I think I would strongly recommend to the Jury that you award Mr. Gilmore his life. Make one other comment about the instructions to the Jury. You'll get to read them when you go into the jury room, and I will encourage you do so. They are very brief. They tell you what you can and cannot consider in determining whether or not you should vote to impose the death penalty; or whether or not you should vote to not impose the death penalty, which would result in a life-imprisonment sentence.

I think the circumstances here are such that you should consider some of the things that are indicated in the mitigating circumstances section of the instructions. I would point out to you, as is indicated in the instructions, that in

74

order to impose the death penalty, it does require a unanimous vote of all twelve of you. If one of you does not vote to impose the death penalty, then the sentence will be life imprisonment, and it will be imposed by the Court as such. I would ask each of you to search your own conscience and to impose, in this case, life imprisonment.

THE COURT: Mr. Esplin, do you care to make any comments?

MR. ESPLIN: I think Mr. Snyder has accurately portrayed my feelings, also, in this, Your Honor. I'm advised by the defendant at this time that he does not wish to make any further statements other than what he's made from the stand.

THE COURT: Is that true, Mr. Gilmore?

MR. GILMORE: Yes, that's true.

THE COURT: You do not desire to make any further statement or further argument to the Jury?

MR .GILMORE: No.

THE COURT: Do you have anything that you'd like to say to the Jury before they retire to deliberate?

MR. GILMORE: Well, I'm finally glad to see they are looking at me. No, I have nothing to say.

THE COURT: Do you have anything further, Mr. Wootton?

MR. WOOTTON: No.

THE COURT: Ladies and Gentlemen of the Jury, you will please then go with the bailiff to the jury room, and take with you the forms that I have prepared, and the instructions, and the one exhibit. Yes. Just one minute. I do want him sworn. Will you please swear him.

(Whereupon, the bailiff was duly sworn to take charge of the Jury.)

THE COURT: Just one minute now before you leave. I want to make it clear to you that one alternative that you have, is to conclude that you do not unanimously render a verdict for death. It isn't that you must all agree to that; but you must conclude that further deliberation would not result in a verdict of death. If you reach that point, or when you reach the point where there is a unanimous verdict for death, then notify the bailiff of your—that you've reached a conclusion, and he'll conduct you into court.

(Whereupon, the Jury retired to deliberate at 4:11 p.m..)

THE COURT: The record will show that the Jury has left the courtroom. Are there any other matters to be taken up before we are notified that their deliberations have been concluded?

MR. SNYDER: Yes, Your Honor, two matters. I think we should state for the record that we have no objections to the instructions given by the Court to the Jury; or whether we do or not, as far as this particular phase of the proceedings; and on behalf of the defendant, I would state that we had none. Furthermore, I would make a motion now that I reserved at the time I objected in the beginning of Mr. Wootton's statement. I think that his referral to the deceased's wife and children is prejudicial—it's unfair. And even after Mr. Wootton commented, he later said: "Think of the position it puts Bennie's wife in." And I wrote that down, I hope accurately, from the comment he had made, even after he had been instructed by the Court. I would further object to Mr. Wootton's comments in closing argument as being prejudicial, the comments and objections with regard to letting him out of prison if he were to receive a life sentence. I think that is also objectionable and prejudicial, and on that basis we move for a mistrial.

MR.WOOTTON: Submit it.

THE COURT: Your motion is denied. We'll be in recess, then, until the Court notifies us that they concluded—or until the Jury notifies us that they have concluded their deliberations.

(Whereupon, the Court recessed at 4:13 p.m., October 7, 1976.)

The jury returned after only one hour and twenty minutes.

THE COURT: The record will show that the Jury has returned; that they are all present and seated in the jury box, that the defendant is present in court represented by his counsel, and that the State of Utah is represented by [the] Utah County Attorney. Dr. Cutler, has the Jury signed one of the documents which you took with you into the jury room?

THE FOREMAN OF THE JURY: (Dr. Virginia Cutler) The Jury has signed.

THE COURT: Would you please hand both, then, to the bailiff? Mr. Clerk, would you please read the verdict?

(Whereupon, the court clerk read the verdict sentenced to death to the Jury.)

THE CLERK: Now, Ladies and Gentlemen of the Jury, would you each answer audibly as I call your name in answer to this question: Was this, and is this, your verdict?

"Yes," was the answer from all twelve jurors.

THE CLERK: Unanimous, You're Honor.

THE COURT: The law provides that at this time the Jury then shall be discharged and the sentence imposed by the Court. Ladies and Gentlemen of the Jury, you have been most attentive in this case, most cooperative with the court personnel pertaining to your personal inconveniences which your jury service has entailed, and, more importantly, you have most conscientiously performed your duty. By your service you have made a significant contribution to the administration of justice, for which the Court thanks you most sincerely. You are discharged. You may remain, however, in the courtroom, if you desire; and you may remain in the seats that you now occupy. But you are discharged as jurors. Now, Mr. Gilmore, if you will please stand. Having been found guilty of the crime of Criminal Homicide, Murder in the First Degree, by a jury of your peers, and that jury having also rendered a unanimous verdict for death, it is now the judgment of the Court that you be put to death in the matter provided by law. Section 77-36-16 of the Utah Code provides that the punishment of death must be inflicted by hanging the defendant by the neck until he is dead, or by shooting him, at his election. If the defendant neglects or refuses to make election, the Court at the time of making the sentence must declare the mode and enter the same as a part of the judgment. Do you have an election as to the mode of death?

MR. GILMORE: I'd prefer to be shot.

THE COURT: Very well, that will be the order. And that will be included as a part of the Court's judgment. Now the law requires me to fix a date for the execution of the sentence, which must not be less than thirty days, or more than sixty days from this date. I fix Monday, November 18th—that's not correct. Monday, November 15th. Monday November 15th, 1976 at eight o'clock a.m. as the date for execution. And you are remanded to the sheriff of Utah County for delivery to the warden of the Utah State Prison, there to be held until execution of the sentence. I advise you, Mr. Gilmore, that you have a right to appeal this conviction and sentence to the Utah Supreme Court. And I appoint the same counsel who have heretofore been appointed to defend you in this matter, to take such steps as they deem appropriate and proper to perfect your appeal to the Supreme Court. In the event of your appeal, the Court will entertain a motion for a stay of execution until such time as the appeal is determined. Are there any other matters to come before the Court at this time—?

MR. WOOTTON: No, sir.

THE COURT: —in connection with this case?

MR. ESPLIN: No, Your Honor.

THE COURT: The Court will be in recess.

(Whereupon, the Court recessed at 6:45 p.m., October 7, 1976.)

Some have said that perhaps his minute exposure to Mormonism inspired this choice to satisfy a belief in blood atonement. I doubt this conjecture. Others said he was afraid a hanging could be botched which might cause longer suffering; this makes more sense to me. Samuel Smith was warden at the Utah State Prison when Gilmore was sentenced.

Utah State Prison

Chapter Four

Aftermath of the Trial

Gilmore's attorneys were preparing the usual course of action after such a verdict. They had every intention of running an appeal, but Gary surprised everyone with his response. He told them he did not want to spend his life on death row and wanted to be executed. I believe to some extent he felt this choice was the ultimate defiance of authority, knowing that no one had been executed for so long he may have doubted it would happen again.

He soon fired his public defenders and hired Dennis L. Boaz, a lawyer from California who had written to Gary in support of Gary's desire to be executed. Boaz had previously moved to Utah, leaving California and his law practice to pursue a career in writing. Utah attorney Tomas A. Jones vouched for Dennis Boaz, a California attorney, so that he could practice in Utah for this one case. Gary requested the services of Boaz as a lawyer, because Boaz was qualified; and thus the deal was done. Boaz later admitted his main objective was to get interviews to write a book and or movie. Gary traded his exclusive interviews and details of his crimes for legal services.

Five years prior to the Gilmore trial, in 1972, the U.S. Supreme Court had ruled the death penalty to be cruel and unusual punishment, making it unconstitutional. All states were ordered to commute death sentences to life imprisonment, meaning no more death row.

In 1975, the Supreme Court made a series of rulings that allowed capital punishment to be reinstated for certain types of murders. As of July 2, 1976, just three weeks before Gary murdered the two men, capital punishment was reinstated. The reinstatement was the easy part. Now getting someone executed was the difficult and final feat.

It had been over ten years since an execution had been carried out in the United States. Gary was supposed to be executed in no less than thirty days of sentencing, but within no more than sixty days of sentencing. There were no provisions for what might happen if Utah failed to execute Gary within this schedule. Some wondered if Gary might go free on a technicality. For example, if he was not executed within the required time, he could possibly be released on a *Writ of Habeas Corpus*, because the only sentence he had received was death. A writ of habeas corpus is an order that requires a detained person be brought before a court to decide the legality of the detention or imprisonment. It had been so long since an execution in Utah, that the state was uncertain that they would be ready in time.

A few days before his scheduled execution, Gary argued his death wish before the Utah State Supreme Court, insisting that he did not want to spend his life on death row. He stated that his sentence was fair and proper, and that he wanted to "accept it like a man."

The thought of an execution stirred the residents of Utah and anti-capital-punishment groups across America. By a vote of four to one, the Justices granted his wish. Over one hundred men volunteered to be on the firing squad.

The protests began. Some activist groups could not abide such a decision on Gary's part, and his former lawyers felt duty-bound to continue to file an appeal. It was said that when Mikal Gilmore, Gary's younger brother, heard that his brother had received the death penalty, he called his mother to tell her about the verdict, saying, "They haven't executed anyone in this country for ten years, and they're not going to start with Gary."

The execution date of November 15, only 38 days after sentencing, came and went. Associations against the death penalty-such as the ACLU - American Civil Liberties Union and the NAACP - National Association for the Advancement of Colored People-anticipated stopping this execution, even though Gilmore was not African American. They did not want a precedent of giving in to a defendant and dispensing with the appeals process.

Many people had an interest in stopping the death penalty in the United States. Obviously people who didn't want the death penalty included most of those criminals who were sentenced to death, as well as future prisoners. Certainly the anti-capital-punishment activists didn't want the Gilmore case to continue in the direction it was going. Despite Gary's protests, a stay of execution was granted by the Governor of Utah Calvin Rampton.

Gary longed for the entire process to be over and was ready to die.

For weeks, Gary and Nicole talked of a dual suicide. She acquired fifty seconal and twenty dalmane which are both a sedative used for sleep disorder or insomnia of which she divided between the two them. Then she smuggled his half, double wrapped in balloons, and hidden in a body cavity.

The death pact was set for midnight. Nicole swallowed her dose, but Gary did not take his at midnight. He waited until near morning to take the pills. Many wondered if perhaps Gary wanted her to die, while he was found and saved. Both survived, and subsequently Nicole was placed in a psychiatric facility.

All contact was then ended between Gary and Nicole. This is when Gary began a hunger strike lasting twenty five days. He would only consume water and black coffee.

This was the second scheduling of the execution. Gary had hoped and expected to be executed on December 8th. He fired Dennis Boaz ending the exclusive interview agreement. Gary and his uncle Vern hired two new attorneys, Ron Stanger and Bob Moody, who spoke on Gary's behalf as he went before the Board of Pardons to plead for death. Gary asked all anti-death-penalty activists to, "Butt out. It's my life and death." He was determined, and his execution was set again, this time for December 6th.

At this time, Lawrence Schiller gained control of access to Gary's story for a book about the case and movie rights.

Five days before Gary's execution, his will was filed with the Fourth District Court. He named his uncle, Vern Damico, as sole beneficiary and executor. The document acknowledged Gary's mother as having a contractual agreement exclusive of the will. His girlfriend Nicole was not included in the will.

On December 3, his mother stepped in. She filed a petition through Richard Giauque, the man who had convinced the Supreme Court to stop capital punishment several years earlier. They were asking the Court to grant Certiorari—a discretionary writ requesting a review.

Learning that his execution would be delayed for the second time, Gary attempted suicide on the morning of December 16, 1976, but again he failed. Gary was taken to the University of Utah Medical Center for treatment after ingesting an overdose of Phenobarbital. He was then kept under hourly surveillance. For a while he was placed in a special isolation cell, until the cost of extra guards forced his return to maximum security. After a prison investigation as to how Gary obtained the Phenobarbital, they reached the conclusion that the drugs were supplied from another prison inmate.

Schiller made a financial agreement with Gary's family and the heirs of the two victims. Soon after, a court battle ensued in which the press petitioned for access to Gary. The battle ended at the Utah Supreme Court, with Schiller losing.

During Gary's prison stay, his story became the object of very competitive bidding rights. When the rights to Gary's story came up for sale, he authorized his Uncle Vern to sell to Lawrence Schiller and to the ABC Network. One source said he received $50,000, another $100,000 and still another said $500,000.00. Gary distributed the money among relatives and former associates from prison. The wife of the second murder victim, Ben Bushnell, filed suit for $2 million. The wife of Jensen sued for one million dollars in addition to fifty thousand dollars for punitive damages. Max Jensen's insurance company filed a third suit for $44,000 for workman's compensation and funeral costs.

The methods used by relatives and the press to gather information from Gary was dictated by the prison authorities.

The prison enforced its terms for the right of relatives to visit, for people to correspond with Gary, and for people to communicate through Gary's attorneys. Lawrence Schiller, a Los Angeles journalist signed with almost anyone who could get through to Gilmore to conduct his interviews. Along with notes from personal interviews, thirty-seven hours of tape-recorded conversations, and around 10,000 handwritten answers to questions directed at Gary.

Gilmore received around two hundred letters a day. He estimated a total of around 7,000 letters while at the prison.

Schiller worked out of a motel room. At odd hours, Gary would call the motel to give him information. Playboy magazine subsequently released an article based primarily on Schiller's interviews.

Many believed Gary might be bluffing about his wish for execution, but he didn't change his mind: He seemed determined to die.

Gary's younger brother Mikal came to Utah to speak with him about stopping the execution. But after talking with Gary, Mikal seemed convinced that Gary knew what he was doing. During their last time together it was said that Gary kissed Mikal on the mouth and then said enigmatically, "See you in the darkness." Mikal left and took no further action to stop the execution.

The night before Gary was to die, he was in good spirits. His Uncle Vern admitted smuggling in some whiskey. Gary's favorite singer, Johnny Cash, called and sang him a song. He had also sent Gary an autographed copy of his autobiography, *The Man in Black*. Gary made a tape recording for Nicole, asking her again to kill herself for him. The warden asked Gary what he might want for his last meal. Gary said, "I don't know; but I would like a couple cans of beer."

Warden Samuel Smith would not disclose the location of the execution to prevent any kind of possible interference. He said the execution would take place somewhere on the 1200 acre property and that was all.

Gilmore invited five people to his execution, two lawyers, his girlfriend, his Uncle, and Schiller the man who bought the rights to his story. Nicole did not attend.

The execution was scheduled the third time for January 17, 1977. In the last hours, a federal court judge in Salt Lake City, U.S. District Judge Willis W. Ritter, ordered a stay. But just as quickly, the 10th Circuit Court of Appeals in Denver lifted the stay of execution that had been granted seven hours earlier by Ritter. Only minutes before dawn, the execution was allowed to proceed as scheduled.

Twenty people witnessed Gary's execution including our family friend and neighbor Utah County sheriff Mack Holley, Utah county prosecuting attorney Noall Wootton, Brent Bullock from the county attorney's office, lawyers Ron Stanger and Bob Moody, and Gary's uncle Vern Damico and others.

At 8:00 a.m. on January 17, 1977, the volunteer firing squad took their places in a cannery warehouse behind the Utah State Prison.

Only four of the five weapons were supposed to be loaded. One rifle would fire a blank; each man could then consider the thought that he might not be the one to take another's life. The firing squad members were paid $100 each. The squad captain received $125. The members were paid in cash so that no records would carry there name. At least, this method is the usual procedure. The barrels of their rifles were placed through holes in a wall.

Gary handed his watch to Vern and asked him to give it to Nicole, who was to set the watch to read the hour and minute of execution, and then to break the watch. He was tightly strapped to a chair, because the slightest movement could make the bullets miss their mark.

In preparing this book, I spoke with Jack Ford the media contact at the Utah State Prison regarding the details of the location of this long-past, famous execution. According to Jack Ford the execution took place in an old building they called the cannery, located behind the prison. "At the time of the execution," Ford related, "they used an old wooden captain's chair."
The cannery has been remodeled and now is being used for furniture construction by the prisoners. The prison has since done a makeover of the chair that is used.

After Gary was placed in the captain's chair, a round target was pinned to his shirt over his heart. Gary then said the now-famous line, "Let's do it." But these were not his last words. They placed a black hood his head. A priest delivered the last rites. Gary spoke again in Latin saying, "Dominus vobiscum" which is Latin for "The Lord be with you." And the countdown began.

Shots rang out. "His head moved slightly to the left, but he stayed erect. His blood then emerged from the black tee shirt and onto his white slacks." Vern later said that after receiving the clothes that Gary was wearing when executed, he found five bullet holes in the shirt. Apparently no one had used a blank, contrary to the usual procedure.

Some of Gary's organs were donated, including his eyes, which sparked a hit song titled, "Gary Gilmore's Eyes," sung by a German punk rock band called the Adverts.

The remains of Gary Gilmore were cremated.

Gary's ashes were scattered in three designated locations in Utah, including where I lived, Spanish Fork. Many watched the sky for Gary's ashes, as Gary Mark Gilmore's execution reopened the door to capital punishment.

The cost of Gilmore's execution was estimated to be $60,000.

Prison Scene Described By Reporter

Editor's Note: Herald reporter Tom Haraldsen was with the press corps inside the State Prison during the night and at the time of the execution today.

By TOM HARALDSEN

Security at the prison was tight and well-planned. Roads surrounding the prison were blocked and protesters diverted out of the area by 4:30 p.m. Sunday. At 5 p.m. the last rays of the sun disappeared from over the prison grounds, the last time Gilmore

GARY GILMORE, convicted slayer whose wish to be executed was granted this morning after final legal barriers were removed. (UPI Telephoto)

Photos from the Daily Herald - Provo, Utah

Gilmore Encounters

Recollections and Opinions

The following are the opinions and memories of people having personal experiences with Gary Mark Gilmore.

Mark
September 12, 2008

Vern, Randy and I were about 17 years old, I'm guessing, maybe a little younger; and we went to the old Albertson's on Center Street in Orem across from the one there right now. We were in his little Volkswagen Beetle looking for someone to buy us beer. So we went into the Albertson's store and saw a gentleman with his back to me standing near the beer coolers, and I said, "Hey." And as he turned around I saw blood running out of his eardrum. Then when he looked at me I just said, "well hey it's all right never mind." I turned and went down the isle to find someone else and he followed me.

He said, "Hey what did you need?"

I said, "Well, we were looking for someone to buy us some beer.

He said, "I won't buy you any, but you can pay me and I'll steal you some."

So I looked at him said "Yaw sure, whatever." So I told Vern to kind of watch the front of the isles and we waited down by the end of the isles; and sure as hell he did, I can't remember what kind of beer it was. But we walked out and put it in the car and we paid him.

Then he kept quizzing us about where's the party and were there going to be any girls there. We told him to get lost, and finally had to tell him to just get the hell out of here. Finally he got the message and he took off.

We partied that night then the following morning, I can't remember, seems like it might have been a Sunday morning; anyway, the next morning Vern, he lived three doors down, he called in a panic, frenzy, and said hey look at the front page of the paper. So I ran outside and grabbed the paper and on the front page was the same guy we had buy us the beer.

Sherrie
September 16, 2008

How I met Gary was that he lived right next door to my best friend Elaine Baum—she is dead now. I was down there all of the time every day. I'm sure she was sick of me, but she never did tell me. Gary and Nichole lived next door; Nichole left often, I don't know where she went, maybe she worked. Gary tended her kids so he would come over to Elaine's yard because it was nice and had grass and he would let the kids play, and he would play with them. Often we would invite him in for coffee, and he would come in the house and have coffee and then go back out to the kids. He was polite and normal; there was nothing wrong with Gary.

One day I was down there and he came over with a huge blown up face, and his eye was closed. And I asked him what happened, and he told me he had gotten into a fight. I told him that "you have got to have some medical intervention, this is a serious thing, you probably don't know this but it looks like you have opened up a window to your brain. You might have a concussion you don't even know it and you need to see a doctor."

He said, "I have no way of seeing a doctor, I have no car, and I have no doctor."

And I said, "Will you go to the emergency room?"

He said "no way," and I told him I would take him. We got into the car and I took him over to Payson Hospital Emergency Room, and I waited for them to give him medical attention. He did in fact have a fracture in his face and or skull; they gave him antibiotics to prevent infection to the brain.

I brought him home, and he was grateful and polite, and I could never dream that Gary would do what he did. When we found out about the murders, Elaine and I were both emotionally involved with it, enough that we wanted to attend his trial. We wanted to go to his trial to give him a little emotional support, because he had never done any harm to us. We didn't visit him in jail, but we did go to the trial.

We arrived and went in, we sat right behind him, and he looked around and acknowledged that we were there. Nichole sat behind us; we listened to the first part of the trial, with him having no defense, with lawyers that he had they had no way to defend him. There was a lunch break and they took him back to jail, Nichole came up to us and asked us to take her down to the jail. I said yes, because I was driving that would be ok, she said that she would find her own way back.

Well she couldn't find her own way back, we waited to see that, and I told her I would pick her up at what ever time. We went down and picked her up.

In the mean time there was a rumor that had circulated in the court that Nichole was there to break Gary out. She had all the plans and everything to break him out. So when we arrived back the security comes and takes our purses, and they scanned us and they took Nichole into a separate room and made her undress, and gave her what ever they do, and strip search. So we went back into the court room listened to the rest of the trial. He had no defense, his lawyers had nothing to say, the prosecutor had a lot to say, and Gary didn't care. You could tell that he didn't care then. The trial ended and we left.

The jury met later that day, we didn't know that, but the jury later that day came to the conclusion that he was guilty. They did give him the death penalty, it was like none other that I have seen, and it was very quick. That was the end of my encounter with either one of them. And for reasons that I still can't figure out, I cried and cried and cried. I don't know what my feelings were toward Gary, but that's my story.

The only other thing I remember is that while he was living there he did the carving in the tree. He did that while he was there, and we saw him doing the carving. He would go out there and carve a little bit at a time. I know that a lot of people came to see it. It said Gary and Nichole inside a heart with an arrow through it.

We knew when he was going to be cremated, Elaine and I knew, I don't know how we knew. We actually knew the day was set to empty his ashes out of the airplane, over the house that he and Nichole shared. We watched for it but didn't see it. We both felt equally bad, and I think related a lot of the same traits to my son Brad. That is why I decided that I cried for him.

Shane

Gary and Nicole used to stop by our house in Mapleton quite often and there was usually a party going on there. We lived on the old highway by the café. Gary was always giving things to people bragging that he had stolen the items. This day he gave a knife to someone at the house while sitting at the Kitchen table. Nicole (his girlfriend) blew up complaining that he never gave her anything. So he pulled another knife out of his pocket and carved his name and the year on one side and hers on the other. We all watched him and chuckled. Then he stood up and said, "Here Nicole, this one is for you." We continued to party for a few hours before Gary and Nicole left. We then discovered the knife had been left on the table. I picked it up and said "look Gary carved the wrong year into the handle." He carved 1975 instead of 1976. He gave us a lot to laugh about but also made us nervous thinking about what he might do next.

Below is a photo of the knife.

Jean

September 22, 2008

I was one of two girls my age in our neighborhood at that time. I think what happened was Nicole had spoken with the church authorities to ask for assistance with child care. Because I didn't know her, I wouldn't have met her in any arena. I had no idea who she was and I think from memory that I was called in and asked if I would help with her kids. I can't remember if she had two or three kids. I remember meeting her, and I remember my twelve year old red flags just going bing, bing, bing, bing, but I didn't listen to them at all. I was pretty good at not listening to them at that age. So I didn't pay any attention and I remember going to tend the kids the first time and he was no where around.

Then the second time I watched her kids it was kind of an all day thing, it was like a Saturday deal. I remember meeting him, he came home with her and he seemed very nice, personable, not at all threatening. Oddly enough my red flags did not go off at all. I do remember one of the first few times I was over there, they had a water heater and the water heater was right in the middle of the kitchen, which I thought was strange, and it had a chain around one of the bottom legs, and it was a relatively long chain right around one of the legs of this water heater. And I remember thinking why would you need a chain because it wasn't securing it to the wall or serving any purpose that I could see. I don't remember them having any pets but I do recall wondering what that was all about.

And I remember she was really, really unstable, she was just a crazy person and she would lose it on one of her kids just right in front of me, and start manhandling these little kids and all that, I remember being horrified and not really knowing what to do because my parents were not like that at all, we didn't even see anything like that in our world. And I remember thinking, "gosh I was asked to do this by the bishop or whoever, and maybe I ought to say something to them or I didn't know whether to say something to my mom," but I knew with the conservatives that I lived with, I thought she would have pulled me from that situation immediately so I didn't. I also thought I don't know quite what to do here and I felt bad for Nicole because it was obvious she was not stable so I just didn't say anything for a while and I remember meeting him on several occasions after that four, five or six times but only the last time did I ever think something is off with this guy.

I remember him coming home really dirty and she was with him, they came home and he was just filthy like he had rolled though the mud, covered in dirt or oil, I don't know what it was. She asked him to walk me home and you know how far that was, not even a half of block and it was dark and he wouldn't do it, he didn't verbally refuse in front of me but he said, "I've got something else to do," and he went in the other room; and that's the last time I saw him. And then I got home and that's the night I decided I need to say something about her behavior. He really never did anything to make me think twice. Except he seemed a little off the last time I was there. I don't know if that was a significant point in time or not. I remember telling my mother because I had came to the conclusion I didn't want to baby sit for her anymore. So I remember telling my mother "this is just a little weird for me."

And she of course was, "well then you just stay away from there!" was the reaction. She called several times after that looking for me to come watch the kids. I believe my mom made it clear to her that that wasn't going to happen and she showed up a couple times after that and I think she was high or drunk or something, you know she was acting really weird. You know as a twelve year old little Mormon girl from Spanish Fork I didn't know how to identify any of that so it could have been anything, at that point it could have been him. So that was just further evidence to me that I had made the right decision.

And then it wasn't too long after that things started coming out. Then I remember my mother of course saying, "oh my goodness." And when it all came out everyone in the whole neighborhood was just freaked out. Nothing like that had ever happened in that area.

Nicole was a cute girl you know petite and cute and her kids were cute, but she was a freak. I remember they were really cute kids and that's what drew me to the situation. They were obviously in need of attention, she seemed very neglectful.

Michael – Attorney
September 24, 2008

My first contact was of course right after he had been arrested within a day or so, I was the public defender down here. I had never done a capital case before not many people had, they hadn't filed any for a long time because of the moratorium. Around that time the Supreme Court approved the death penalty again which was brought about by three cases. They filed Gilmore's as a capital case because there were two murders even though he was only charged with one.

I remember entering the prison was interesting we had to go through the main gate then through two separate locked doors into the room they brought Gilmore in to meet with us. Craig Snyder was my co attorney on the case. We said to each other if Gilmore wanted to get us by the time the guard could get out of his protective room it would be to late. But we never had any problems with Gary. He used to draw and was pretty good. He also wrote poetry and a lot of letters. Sometimes in his letters and poems you could tell if he had been interrupted and annoyed by the guards or someone because the attitude in his writing would change. He didn't like being disciplined or told what to do.

Kenny 12/12/08

I met Gary Gilmore while working in Lindon, Utah at a bar called Fred's Lounge or as we use to call it "the knife and gun club." I would occasionally bartend but usually I worked the door collecting a cover charge for the band so I knew most of the people who frequented the bar. Gary always stood out in a crowd he liked to have attention most of the time. He had a way of making his presence known and generally if there was trouble while he there his was part of it. He would usually stop in a couple times a week. Many of the times he stopped in he was trying to sell different things and we all knew most of the items were probably stolen but he wasn't the only one doing this. I especially remember when he was trying to sell some guns; it had to be the ones he had stolen from Swan's market.

His Uncle Vern Damico was my sister's landlord so I knew him well and considered him a good guy. Vern tried to help Gary over and over again but just couldn't get through to him, he lacked social skills he was very impatient and a terrible temper when he wanted something he wanted it now. If he didn't get his way he would blow up. Although he wasn't dumb in fact he seemed quite intelligent. He was very jealous of Nicole or whoever he was trying to date at the time.

Sometimes he would come in and just be a regular guy but he wasn't afraid to approach people about selling items. The big draw to this bar was the pool tables and betting on the games. Gary was a poor loser especially after he got a few drinks in and started believing he was unbeatable and invincible. It didn't take us long to figure him out so everybody just played his game. The owner, Fred, had to tell to back off and calm him down when he was trying to sell guns out in the parking lot.

I never did see him get in any fights while at the bar I only saw him get upset and slam a few beer bottles down on the bar. But we always felt the need to keep on eye for him. We had a much diversified crowd everything from the Sundowners motorcycle gang to Polynesian and Mexican gangs. It's surprising we didn't have more trouble than we did but the police stopped by most every night.

My ex-wife worked evenings at the City Center motel as the desk clerk and was scheduled to work the night Gary murdered his second victim. Her friends had called her earlier and asked her to go out with them. It has always bothered her, felt guilty that she took that night off of work because she wonders whether or not he would have killed her. She thought being a woman that perhaps he might not have murdered her.

I remember later when the movie company came and filmed at the bar. Fred Junior and some of us were in the background when filming the movie, The Executioners song.

The fact that Gary refused his appeals and dared the court to execute him was so far from the norm that it made a very rare case. I believe he did feel bad about what he had done but just couldn't control himself at times. He always seemed antsy he should have been called itchy he was always moving. Many of the Provo city police department already knew Gary by the time he committed the murders from many other various smaller crimes. He could be very friendly and likeable when he was in the right mood.

Chapter Five

Murder Still Echoes

Twenty-three years after the Gilmore tragedy, I opened and operated a combination golf-and-pawn shop in Spanish Fork, Utah. Utilizing the skill of building and repairing golf clubs taught to me by my father and began learning the anomalous trade of a pawn broker. Not long after opening the store, I added the bail bonding business, having soon realized that a lot of the people pawning items and needing bail bonds were the same clientele.

At this time, the cowboy boots of my choice were made of butterscotch-colored lizard skin. They were comfortable, durable, and stylish to the point of natty. After all, I was a businessman.

My shop, called "Aim High Golf and Pawn," was located on Main Street in Spanish Fork, Utah. The business itself was a long shot—featuring short capital—and it taught me a lot about the long and short of both business and people. It also gave me an insider's knowledge of collectible firearms and an intimate knowledge of the Gilmore Gun.

The business began to grow, along with some headaches and heartaches. Pawning is tough businesses to be in if you are too compassionate. It's difficult to help everyone as much as you or they would like, while covering overhead and trying to make a profit. When pawning, for some reason, many people feel obligated to tell you why they need the money, and then comes "the story." My particular location gave me a view of the only liquor store and bar in town, which shot a lot of holes in "the stories." It's none of my business what others do with their money, and I'd rather not know rather than listen to a lie.

When the store opened I was divorced at the time, with my only child helping me operate the store. He was about a year and a half old and has stuck with me through it all.

It was a unique shop. You might have walked in to see me changing my son's diaper on my desk, or holding him with a bottle in his mouth. As quirky as it sounds I wouldn't change that time together for anything.

A few months after opening I applied for and received a FFL (Federal Firearms License} Firearms are a big part of the pawn business, especially in states such as Utah. Acquiring numerous guns, I occasionally began selling on internet gun auctions and gun shows in the western states. I've been interested in guns since I was a child, so I really enjoyed the exposure to so many firearms. But having been struck by buckshot to my face during a hunting trip when I was sixteen, I also had a healthy respect for what firearms could do to a person when in the wrong hands.

My shop was just four blocks north of where Swan's Market had existed twenty-four years prior. Swan's Market had played a pivotal role in the criminal career of Gary Gilmore. He had stolen eleven guns from Swan's, including the "Gilmore Gun," the murder weapon.

Gordon Swan was the owner of that popular little store, sort of a mini Wal-Mart, selling about everything you could ever need. The junior high school was across the street, which made the market a popular teen hangout. It was open late and on Sundays. I've known Gordon and his family since childhood. Not only was Gordon a good businessman, but also a talented artist and a friendly guy with a good sense of humor.

Gordon's daughter Judy, worked at the city court in Spanish Fork, and we became reacquainted while I often stopped by the court to work on bail bonds. One day, the subject of the Gilmore Gun came up. She asked if I remembered the case and mentioned to me that her father still had the murder weapon.

I didn't know until then and was amazed the gun had been returned to Gordon after the trial, up until now I thought it customary that weapons used in murder cases were destroyed by the police. The research I've done has verified this custom for the most part. The fact that the gun was returned was a very rare incident. Judy asked if I would be interested in perhaps selling the gun at a show. I replied, "Have your father stop by the shop and we'll talk about it."

The Gilmore Gun
Browning pistol used by Gary Mark Gilmore for two
murders.

A few weeks later, Gordon stopped by with his wife
Barbara, daughter Judy, and her husband Barry. We came to
an agreement: I'd sell the gun for a percentage of the net
profit. It was June, 2001; and when the Swans showed up to
talk, they brought quite a collection of newspaper articles and
documents concerning and authenticating -the firearm.

After our agreement, and for the following few weeks, I
struggled with my feelings. Before I'd even made the
agreement, I had discussed the subject with my family and
friends: should I decide to help the Swans sell the gun? Most
people felt the same as I did—that it was a rare item, and in
spite of the tragedy Gilmore caused, the case had helped
serve an important historical purpose. This is when I coined
the name "Gilmore Gun."

Now, having the Gilmore Gun in my possession, the publicity, memories and reality of what had happened years before came back to haunt me.

Court returns guns stolen by Gary Gilmore.
Photos from the Daily Herald - Provo, Utah

In meeting with the Swans, I learned many details about the crime known personally to them and not known to the public. For example, Gordon said that Norman Mailer telephoned him before writing the book *The Executioner's Song*, asking Gordon around one hundred and fifty questions. After reading the book, Gordon found that Mailer hadn't used much of the facts from the interview. Mailer also promised him a book which he never received.

Thus, there are several crucial and chilling facts that I was able to learn from Gordon and Barbara Swan that have not been made public about Gary's brazen thefts:

"Gilmore often came in the store, but we didn't know who he was until later."

Many store clerks in other stores remembered Gary coming in and picking up a six packs of beer and other items, then walking out without paying. They said "he had such a mean look on his face they didn't dare say anything to him."

"We, Swans Market, were robbed five times. But the one we dreaded the most was while we were gone camping in the Uinta Mountains. Gilmore broke into the store at about 2:30 a.m. and took eleven guns out of our cases. First he took them outside to his truck. He then took the guns out of the boxes leaving them on the ground, and put the guns in a gunny sack. He had been in the store previously and knew where and what to take."

"We wondered how he knew we were out of town when he robbed our store or if it was just luck." This question was never answered.

"Our home was connected to the store. Nine of the eleven guns stolen were returned after Gary's trial, including the murder weapon."

About a week later after stealing the weapons, Gary returned and was casing the store again, asking what we had and the prices. He hung around too long for comfort. Finally he bought a six-pack of beer and left. At least, we thought he had left.

A while later Steve, Gordon's son, helped carry groceries out to a lady customer's car. He spotted Gary still sitting out front in his truck. Steve asked, 'What's the matter? Won't your truck start?"

Gary stammered for a moment and responded, "Ah— uh—no, it won't start."

Steve asked if he needed a push to help start it. Gary said, "Yes."

Steve pushed the truck for about a block and a half down a street that grew darker, but Gilmore never let the clutch engage to start the engine of the truck.

Steve became suspicious and apprehensive telling Gilmore he had to get back to the store. Thank goodness he did. Later that night Gilmore robbed and murdered his first victim in Orem."

Barbara Swan was a nurse at the hospital in Provo, which gave her a close perspective on the tragic relationship between Gary and Nicole. While Gary was incarcerated after the murders, Gary and Nicole planned a pact where both would attempt suicide. As mentioned earlier they failed, and Nicole was under Barbara's care at the hospital. After pumping Nicole's stomach, Barbara stated she felt the dosage had been too small to be lethal. She believed Gary and Nicole were aware that the dosage was insufficient. Barbara and the other nurses caring for Nicole said that out of all the people they had given care to, "Nicole was the most difficult. Uncooperative and demanding," but commented Nicole was very knowledgeable in the use of profanity."

"Gilmore was classified ADD (attention deficit disorder)," Barbara said. "He did have a talent for art and drew pictures of Nicole that were quite good. But he seldom drew when not incarcerated. Because of the ADD, he couldn't sit still."

He demanded attention, and did illegal and amoral acts to achieve others awareness. Some said after committing these wrong acts, he sometimes felt the need to repent. This partly explains his desire to be executed after committing murder, according to Mr. Swan.

"While talking with the police officer who returned the guns to us, Gordon told him, "I wish we would have been home when he burglarized the store." He replied, "It was probably a good thing you were gone, or you might be dead now."

"The officer also said, 'I guess you are going to sell the murder weapon." I asked if he would like to buy it. He said, "Yes. But I couldn't pay the price you want or could get for it."

Shortly after the gun was returned to the Swans, a friend of both the Swans' and mine, named Morgan Coombs, took it to a gun show in Las Vegas. While showing the gun around he met an interested collector from Los Angeles, California. The collector asked how much he wanted. Morgan told him $30,000 and the collector offered $20,000.00. Morgan refused and proceeded to show the gun around further. Later, Morgan returned to the collector and asked if he was ready to buy the gun at $30,000.00. The collector again offered

$20,000.00. Morgan refused to haggle or lower the price denying the offer again.

After arriving home, Morgan told Gordon about the interested perspective buyer. Morgan had the collectors' contact information, so Gordon called the collector in California and told him that he was the actual owner and would accept $25,000.00 for the pistol. The collector stated that if the guy at the show would have suggested $25,000.00 he would have bought it; but that he had become offended when the seller wouldn't meet him halfway. Now he was angry and not interested.

Gordon stashed the Gilmore Gun for the next twenty-four years before bringing the pistol to me.

Our town was not the same for quite some time after the murders. Even though Gary had been apprehended in a relatively short time, people working alone at night in gas stations and stores couldn't help being afraid, remembering those who had been killed so easily. Anyone who works as a cashier realizes the possibilities of being robbed and harmed when working alone; but until it happens nearby, to someone you know it doesn't seem as probable.

It was a shocking crime to our area and to the nation. Even Gary believed that he should be put to death. To be sure, there were some activists against the death penalty, who believed Gary should not be executed. But these people weren't in our town and didn't know the terror Gary had caused us, what he had done to our peace of mind. For some time after, the Gilmore Gun loomed in our thoughts and no one felt safe.

Today, perhaps, in the era after 9/11, the public is more aware that there can be evil people in our midst who must be stopped, permanently. Sometimes we must protect ourselves, and this job isn't always pretty.

I'm reminded of the movie Old Yeller, which came out in 1957. The movie was about a yellow lab called Yeller. Yeller was Lassie on steroids. None of this finding-the-kid-lost-in-the-valley stuff for him. No, Yeller fought bears, gathered wood, and dragged the injured home at the very least. In the end of the story, Yeller gets rabies and had to be put down. It's a movie not often shown today, probably because adults wonder if children should see that sometimes we must protect ourselves; and that this task, while necessary, is emotionally painful. It is a sorry fact that killers and terrorists must be put down before they bite you.

As survivors of the Gilmore crime aftermath, the majority of the people I knew in our town were in favor of capital punishment. I remember talking with family friend and neighbor, Sheriff Mack Holley. At the time of the murders, he was the head of the Utah County Sheriff's department. He delivered Gilmore's death warrant to the judge and witnessed the execution. He said that he believed the sentence would serve as a deterrent to further murders and was "Something that had to be done. It was not a pleasant thing to witness; but I feel that our system was on trial, and he had to be executed."

THE ABOVE FOUR MEN, three of them from Provo, were witnesses today to the execution of Gary Gilmore, at the latter's request. From left, top, Vern Damico, Provo businessman, Gilmore's uncle; Larry Schiller, the man who paid $100,000 for the rights to Gilmore's story. From left, bottom, two Provo attorneys, Ronald Stanger and Robert Moody, who legally represented the killer. Apparent-ly Gilmore was legally allowed to request five witnesses. It was reported he had chosen his girlfriend, Nicole Barrett, as the fifth, but she remained today in the Utah State Hospital where she was committed some time ago. Utah State Hospital Superintendent Roger Kiger, when questioned on the matter, replied he is under court orders not to discuss her case in any way.

Top left - Gilmore's uncle Vern Damico
Top right - Larry Schiller writer/reporter
Gary Gilmore's final attorneys
Bottom left - Ronald Stanger
Bottom right - Robert Moody

Photos from the Daily Herald - Provo, Utah

Chapter Six

Pistol with a Past

Now having possession of the Gilmore Gun began the process to determine its "past life" and monetary value, a task any experienced seller must undertake.

The weapon is a Browning Challenger II, semi-automatic pistol. The caliber is a .22 long rifle.

While wracking down the ownership history of the pistol, I discovered that it had passed through multiple hands before it found its way into the hands of a psychopath. Gordon had ordered it from a sales representative who was a Spanish Fork resident. That resident purchased guns from a wholesaler in Grand Junction, Colorado then he sold to businesses. The Colorado wholesaler got the gun from a distributor in Ogden, Utah. The distributor had ordered the pistol direct from the manufacturer, which was Browning Arms, located in Morgan, Utah.

Obviously that resident never got a chance to get it from Swan, because Gary took it when he burglarized the store, stealing the eleven handguns which included the Gilmore Gun.

What use the pistol was destined for could not have been foreseen by any of the people who had it prior to Gary. The consequences and historical events to follow were inconceivable, beginning with the theft and tragic use of this firearm. Although the robbery of the Swans could be calculated into dollars and cents the havoc wrought by one psychopath on the townspeople, from terror to murder, cannot be measured in monetary value.

I had to start somewhere to establish a dollar value to the Gilmore Gun. Being familiar with internet auctions, it seemed the logical place to start, so I proceeded to search the net for another firearm with similar characteristics. There were none. True there have been more famous victims but none that legally or politically compare. No other firearm had been involved in a case legally affecting everyone in the United States at such a high echelon: life and death.

I talked with quite a few authorities concerning various types of guns. Nearly everyone wondered and asked the same question, "How did you get it?" That's a reasonable question. The Gilmore case being such a historical one, and the fact that the gun was released back to Gordon after the trial— well, this course of events seldom happens, which potentially makes this particular handgun a valuable commodity.

I considered eBay auctions, of course, and discovered that they don't allow firearms. I contacted numerous internet auctions and spoke with some of the world's largest auction houses. The common response was, "No precedent is comparable," and "We don't have a category for such an item." So the Gilmore Gun just isn't like other collectible guns that auction houses are used to seeing.

I contacted Butterfield's of San Francisco, one of the world's oldest and best-known auction houses. They have

116

multiple auction houses around the world. However I then learned that just six months prior, eBay had become their partner. They had recently changed their past rules about firearms and would now not allow this pistol, saying that because it was not fifty years old, it wasn't considered an antique. But they would, however, allow antique, curio, and/or relic classified guns. I'll explain the curio and relic classification later.

The gentleman I spoke with at Butterfield's was quite intrigued with the pistol and asked a lot of questions. He also stated he personally was disappointed with the present change of rules, saying that, "a weapon of this historical nature would be very valuable and difficult to price."

I had been selling guns on multiple internet auctions for some time. One of my favorite websites was and still is Gunbroker.com.

Continuing my research, I still had no idea where to start the bidding. I set the opening price at $500,000.00 with bidding at $1,000.00 increments.

The gun received a bid at the opening price. But on this particular auction, the bid needed to be one bid higher than the opening price to be valid. This rule would have made the price $501,000.00 I researched the feedback of the bidder, and the results were favorable with numerous transactions. I attempted to contact the bidder but I received no response.

While sitting in my store one particular day, I was wearing a pair of black striped python snake skin with a grey-toned upper cowboy boots. They are very durable and comfortable without being constricting. I continued contacting other gun dealers while gathering more information.

My weapon of choice to carry at this time was a Baby Eagle semi-automatic in the .40 caliber. This pistol has a great feel—not too large, and well-balanced. The deep concealment choice was a mini five-shot .22 magnum revolver made by North American Arms, a gun that fit well in my boot for a back up in case of an emergency while pursuing bail skips, a robbery while at my shop or whatever undesirable surprising might occur.

Most dealers I spoke with were of the same mind-set— amazed that the gun had been released from the court after the trial. All the while I continued receiving more emails, questions, and offers concerning the pistol. In the midst of my assessing the value of the Gilmore Gun, I did not guess that my shop was being assessed by some desperate addicts. It's a story that shows how close-knit our town was; and that factor provides insight to how the Gilmore crimes could touch an entire small town. In our town, many times everyone knew everything about everybody.

One hot day in July 2001, two women and their children entered my shop. The young women were dressed in low-cut shirts, unbuttoned to the point of being quite revealing. They took turns leaning over my desk to show themselves off to their best advantage. One asked if I would come out to the truck to look at some items too heavy for them to carry into the store that they wanted to pawn. I went out with them to look at these items while leaving some of their children in the store. After returning inside, we talked for a few minutes and they left in a bit of a hurry, without any transactions.

That night, while locking the jewelry in the safe, I noticed that the largest diamond ring was gone from the display tray.

The ring's owner had pawned the ring and asked if I would try to sell it. The ring had a full one-karat diamond. I searched for hours, wondering where the ring might have fallen, but didn't see it anywhere. For many days later, I continually stressed-out about where the diamond ring could have gone.

One morning a regular customer came in and we began to talk. He asked, "Have you lost a diamond ring lately?" Startled, I replied, "Yes, how did you know?" It turns out that he lived next to a popular hamburger joint. As he sat on his front porch, he was able to hear much of the kids' conversation next door. He had overheard a young girl, about twelve, saying that her mother had made her steal a diamond ring from a shop called Aim High. She also said that her mother repeatedly made her purchase illicit drugs and bring the drugs to her. My customer not only recognized the girl, but also knew her name.

Like a good citizen, he had gone over to the burger joint and confronted the child. She began crying and told him everything. So now that I had her name, I went to work.

It just so happened I knew a woman who was a long-time acquaintance of the mother of the twelve-year-old girl. My friend contacted the mother, told her that I was aware of her crime, and threatened that she had better come clean. The ring was soon returned which was quite a lucky instance. If this would have been in a large city chances are the ring would never been found.

You might have wondered if stolen property ever ends up at pawn shops. Yes, and of all the probably stolen property that was pawned in my store, I'd bet that 99 percent was stolen by family, friends of family, and employees. They are the ones who know what you have and where your valuables can be found. A large percentage of thieves trying to pawn items are using drugs, and theft is how they finance their habit.

While contacting other dealers about the value of historical guns, I discovered the term "murderabilia," meaning items that are murderer-related. This term pertains more to personal items, such as photos, clothing, hair, or art done in prison. Personally, I and many others do not consider this gun "murderabilia"; rather a historical piece.

After a phone conversation with an interested antique gun dealer from Arizona, I met with the dealer at a gun show at the Flamingo Casino in Las Vegas, Nevada. He and another firearms dealer from the United Kingdom discussed the pistol at length with me. They were very impressed with the Gilmore Gun, especially the documentation authenticating the gun. They stated the difficulty of pricing an item this rare, but they believed that the value would be very high. All the display tables at this gun show were already booked, so the gun wasn't shown.

In January 2002, the weapon was first displayed at the OKC or Oklahoma City gun show in the Cashman Center in Las Vegas, Nevada.

After short consideration, my choice of footwear had to be the large quill-ostrich cowboy boots in the color of butterscotch, a statement of haute couture.

The following items were included with the Gilmore exhibit:

1. The Gilmore Gun – A browning Challenger II – semi automatic pistol - .22 LR caliber.

2. Norman Mailer's book, *"The Executioner's Song."*

3. The video, *"The Executioner's Song"* starring Tommy Lee Jones and Rosanne Arquette.

4. FBI lab reports identifying the pistol.

5. A Browning Museum examination document.

6. The A&E movie "A Fight to Die" The story of Gilmore's trial and execution.

7. The book by Gary's brother, Mikal Gilmore, titled *"Shot in the Heart."*

8. Numerous newspaper articles regarding the crime.

9. An affidavit from the Utah County Attorney's Office identifying and authenticating the pistol.

Most people do not read the displays very closely. They would repeatedly walk on by keeping the sales pitchers behind their tables at a safe distance while avoiding eye contact. This is typical at most kinds of shows. But occasionally a person would read and realize what the items were; when this happened, the person would then call the others of their group back to take a closer look.

During the first day of the show someone from the *Review-Journal*, the prominent Las Vegas newspaper, called and asked for an interview. They had received telephone calls about this uncommon display. I agreed to do an interview later that day during the show.

In reading the article after it was printed, I saw that they had an incorrect explanation about the $500,000.00 internet bid. Recall that I could not accept the $500,000.00 bid, because the auction rules were that the bid had to be $501,000.00 and that my effort to then contact the bidder had failed. Despite what really happened regarding the bid, the Las Vegas news article reported that I turned down $500,000.00 for the Gilmore Gun. This made for better press.

The response to the Vegas news article was amazing. Throughout the show I met attendees who said that they had come to the show only to see the Gilmore Gun.

The article had been titled, *"Dealer Hawking Gun with a Past,"* and the subtitle announced: "FBI authenticates pistol as weapon used by Utah killer Gilmore in 1976 slayings." The article tells that the pistol was being shown on the twenty-fifth anniversary of the execution of Gilmore, perpetrator of one of the most high-profile cases in the nation's history. It described me and the pistol, with the incorrect statement that I turned down $500,000 for the Gilmore Gun in an internet auction. The article provided a brief history of the case, such as Gilmore being the first person executed in a decade and some of his famous last words, "Let's do it."

I also gave a television interview which aired on the eleven o'clock news. The news also went out on radio, the Associated Press and United Press International. The next morning the telephone began to ring and ring.

People wanted answers and interviews. Many friends called just to say they had seen me on television. The exposure was extraordinary. My younger sister said she heard a radio talk-show host saying, "What idiot would turn down half a million dollars for the gun?" And, "How much does he think it is worth?" There were numerous calls from newspapers. Subsequently, I was interviewed by all the prominent newspapers in Utah.

Naturally, while I was there in Las Vegas, I drove out to the Primm Resort to see the car Bonnie and Clyde were driving when they were gunned down. The historic value of that car reminds me a lot of the essence of the Gilmore Gun. Each year tens of thousands of people stop to view the car, which is riddled with bullet holes. Rumor has it that they can't even put a value on it.

When you stop and consider it, almost all historical events are connected with tragedy, and always at someone's expense. Without tragedy, it's just another common event. Just think of all the war relics on display, practically everywhere you go. Tragedy or victory is determined by which side of the battle your "team" participated on.

Later in March 2002, I made a trip to Del Mar, California for a gun show. The cowboy boots of my choice were the chocolate colored bull shoulder because of the loose comfortable fit for the long drive; in addition to being very comfy, they were subtly exotic. I did not want to look ordinary.

While in Las Vegas, I wanted to speak with a few casinos about the gun and the possibility of some type of promotion. Times have changed; years ago in Las Vegas, you could talk to managers and owners, without all the gatekeepers. Now casinos are just another corporation; cold and removed. I also thought perhaps while in route to Del Mar the Primm Resort might have an interest in the Gilmore Gun. Because, as mentioned before that resort has the Bonnie & Clyde car, so I spoke with them. After speaking with the director of the Primm's promotions, he asked me to get back to him in a few days.

I proceeded to the Del Mar gun show in California. On the drive to the show there were some incredibly strong winds. The road was detoured because of tractor trailers and motor homes being blown over.

When I finally arrived at the gun show it wasn't very busy but the pistol received the usual interested and surprised responses. Like me no one had ever heard of the Gilmore Gun being released back to the Swans. The crime being so long ago the younger people at this show and a few others were not familiar with all the details. I explained the story of the weapon being put away for the last twenty-five years and being recently rediscovered, etc.

On the return trip from Del Mar, I stopped again for the night at the Primm Resort to talk further with the fellow in promotions. The next day he said "All but one of the decision makers are in favor; check back, perhaps later." The grueling drive was around fifteen hundred miles round trip leaving on a Friday night and returning Sunday.

Chapter Seven

Coast to Coast with the Gilmore Gun

The research continued on the Gilmore Gun along with displaying it at only four gun shows. The pistol was shown in Sacramento, California; Reno, Nevada; Salt Lake City, Utah; and Phoenix, Arizona.

Certainly some gun vendors complain that modern gun shows are now less about guns and are becoming more like a flea market. You'll see toys, jewelry, jerky, arts and crafts. I do like some of these booths, but can see the point of the gun-related vendors. As for those vendors next to my space, I was pleased that many told me that they enjoyed having an item as rare and unusual as the Gilmore Gun close by. The gun certainly did attract people to our aisle, and it encouraged the attendees to stop and look. Most of those viewing my display were astonished to see such an historic item, and most people aged forty-five or over were very familiar with the Gilmore case. Some people stopped by who had a friend or a family member involved in a murder case, and wanted to discuss the story of their tragedy. I wish I had recorded them all.

There's a terrific gun show called "The Big Reno Gun Show" in Reno, Nevada. I usually had one particular friend or my father that helped when needed, but this one I worked alone. The booth assigned to me was located between two helpful gentlemen. It is always good to have someone you can trust to watch your booth when nature calls. This show was at the Hilton Hotel Casino and hosted many vendors with primarily gun-related items.

A pair of cream-colored boots with wing-tipped, dark-oak lizard-skin toes arrived just in time for me to wear for this show. After ordering this special custom-made boot, it was four months until delivery; but well worth the wait. They not only have a very impressive look but are still comfortable enough to wear for hours of dancing.

My table was located next to a knife and sword dealer on one side and a fellow from Las Vegas, who said he only did an occasional show on the other side. The occasional vender had only a few guns for this show and said that his usual work was organizing corporations for profit and nonprofit status. We had a very enjoyable conversation as I had been previously securities licensed I'm interested in stocks, bonds, and finances, and he was knowledgeable about these type of business procedures.

For that show, I had also brought a high-end, custom-built rifle that was a real eye-catcher. It was created by two of the well known gunsmiths from the west. The rifle drew a lot of attention. The knife dealer next to me was a humorous, laid-back guy. He was unrivaled in the number of jokes he could pull off the top of his head, which made for an entertaining weekend. He was an early starter on the daily cocktails and it showed by the end of the day.

Another exhibitor admired the Gilmore Gun repeatedly for the multi-day event. He was fascinated with the history and documentation, but remarked that the price was out of his range. He told me of a doctor he knew from southern California who might be interested and that he would surely tell him about the pistol. He also said this doctor had a hidden room of valuable guns behind the bar in his home. Some of his collector's items had belonged to Jesse James and other well-known persons. Was it a tall tale? I didn't hear from the doctor, so perhaps my card was lost.

Not long after returning from the show, a fellow came into my store carrying a couple of rifles. He was a rough-looking character, apparently accustomed to living life through experimental chemistry. He had all the charm and appeal of an unflushed toilet. Tell me, who could ask for a better job than one like being a pawn broker; employment that in my case required sitting alone in a store where dysfunctional people can legally walk in carrying firearms? He asked what I would give him for the rifles. After a close inspection I quoted him what I could pay, he instantly became hostile. I explained they were in terrible condition. The metal was rusty and pitted; the stocks were dinged and scratched, with very little finish left. He stormed out angry. A couple of hours later the phone rang and a voice said, "I'm going to get you. You're going to die." I recognized the voice as the man who had left my store earlier. It is not the kind of phone call that is easily forgotten. But I'm still here. Nothing more ever came of the threats.

As I continued to place the pistol on an occasional internet auction I received constant emails with the same question: "How did you get this gun?" The occasional derogatory email was received of the following variety: "You are crazier than Gary Gilmore to try to sell a gun for that price." Seems the world is full of self-proclaimed experts.

It's interesting how people's opinions change over time from a position of mockery to one of awe, because they begin to realize that they've seen a historic item. Such an incident occurred at one of the gun shows I attended. A particular fellow was a regular vendor at most of the shows and brandished a very large collection of collectible and standard firearms. Others had commented favorably on his knowledge of firearms. He had looked at my exhibit and the Gilmore Gun, making a couple of negative remarks such as "Who would want a gun like that?" Then later the same day, while waiting in line at the concessions, I overheard him saying to others, "Did you see the Gilmore murder pistol?—that gun is priceless." I had to chuckle.

Offers and bids continued, including one at $75,000.00 on another internet auction. The bidder was from Oregon. Gordon considered selling, but the buyer didn't come through.

It was now spring and we had a late snow storm. A friend Steve Shepherd and I were on our way to a gun show in Salt Lake City, about fifty miles away. My son and I picked him up in Springville, a nearby town. As you leave Utah Valley and enter Salt Lake Valley, there is a small mountain pass that we call, "the point of the mountain." Just past the summit is also where both the men's and women's state penitentiaries are located. When crossing the point of the mountain the wind is usually blowing harder and the weather is worse. And today was no different.

We were just approaching where Gary Gilmore's ghost is said to have taken up residence. Suddenly snow appeared on the interstate. There were three lanes in each direction. We were traveling in the fast lane as I glanced to my right just in time to see an out-of-control tractor trailer strike us on the passenger side. Just prior to impact I braced myself with all my might. The impact sent us spinning across the median and into the oncoming three lanes of busy traffic. With three to four inches of snow on the road, the oncoming traffic didn't have much more control than we did. As we spun across the highway, cars were coming directly at us. I was sure we were going to be hit again, but we were repeatedly missed by inches. Our survival still baffles me. As we slid to a stop off the other side of the interstate, I quickly turned to check on my son, who was in his car seat in the rear of the car. He was calmly looking around and said, "Daddy, car off road." I laughed and cried at the same time. Then I asked my friend, Steve, how he was. He said, "I think I'm fine."

Not long after that day a friend named Charlie, who knew that I had the Gilmore Gun, contacted me saying that he had a possible buyer and that he wanted to talk about his commission. But the full story was not revealed until about a month later. He said he had been to a concert and that he had spoke with the singer from the rock band KoЯn saying that he wanted the gun at two hundred fifty thousand. I did do some research and found that band member Jonathan Davis was supposedly a collector of historical macabre items and was opening a museum in California. I told Charlie to arrange it, but didn't hear back.

Just a few weeks later, we received another offer. I called Gordon and asked if he was interested, but told him I didn't think it was enough; so we turned that offer down.

About this time I began speaking with some gun museums. Most were very interested, but they wanted me to donate the pistol to their museum, which I could not do because I was not the owner. More time passed and another fellow I knew contacted me with an offer from a friend of his who wanted to remain anonymous. I phoned Gordon again and asked if he was interested. He decided to accept the offer.

I met with Gordon before connecting with the buyer to cover a few details. Gordon mentioned that he had family in the hospital and could use some money now. So I gave him money out of my pocket as a down payment to help him out. I waited for weeks and never heard from the friend or the supposed buyer. At this point, I was deeply connected with the history of the Gilmore Gun and decided to purchase the pistol myself. Having spent so much time and money on the Gilmore Gun project, I felt it was the right thing to do. I had hoped for the possibility of opening a youth center if I could parlay this rare pistol into enough capital.

When I was a boy growing up my father did a lot for the youth in the community. For years after working all day at the Geneva Steel plant he would take a car load of us kids thirty miles to a boxing gym where he helped coach me and other boys. He also opened an archery club giving free instruction to who ever was interested. After years of bailing out acquaintances, friends and the children of friends I realized the need for people to have somewhere to go and something to do. I admire those who donate their time and appreciate those who give money to help others. I hope to do more of both.

Many people told me to go east to expedite the sale of the Gilmore Gun. "Go to New York, that's where the money is." I had never been to New York City, but I considered a trip there both a possibility and an adventure. I have always preferred doing business in person, rather than by phone or through email. Doing business in person seems to be a dying act, and it is an art. I prefer meeting and looking into a person's eyes when doing business generally trusting my feelings about someone when using this method.

In the spring of 2003, I flew to Baltimore, Maryland, rented a car, and drove to New York after visiting some old friends in the DC area. You can certainly make better time when driving in the West. I had no idea how much time and money was needed to satisfy the toll-booth syndrome.

Driving in New York City is a true test of patience and concentration. One test I hope to now avoid forever. After pricing the hotels in Manhattan I decided to stay in Queens using the subway and taxis to travel. Some of the graffiti art that I saw on buildings while riding the subway was very impressive, but it's a shame the talent is wasted on other's property.

Manhattan is an amazing sight. All the history and familiar buildings I had seen in movies and magazines converged in a montage of energy and excitement—an amusement park for the senses.

I visited Christie's and Sotheby's auction houses. I'm told that these auctions are among the largest in the world. They seemed interested and surprised at what I had to offer. But apprehensive to auction the item, saying that they didn't have a classification for that sort of artifact; and that because of New York's gun laws, the sale might be too prohibitive. I assumed most had no idea what the local laws were, finding out later that I was correct.

The "gatekeepers" were as far as I could get without an appointment, so it's hard to say who they were speaking with on their telephones. It could have been the custodian. I also visited some custom gun shops and viewed some of the most beautiful firearms I've ever seen. Although, at best, in these posh stores I was treated like an intruder, since I wasn't wearing a tux.

Manhattan is one of the most interesting, busiest cities I've been to. But they just didn't seem to be impressed by my cowboy boots and jeans. Looking back, perhaps the wrong boots were worn on this trip. The short-quill ostrich in dark brown with the walking heel might have been better. Although while walking through a certain part of the city the people did become very friendly. For a few moments I felt darn handsome, and then realized the sociable women were prostitutes and the men were gay. Of course, I refused all offers.

I have always enjoyed comedy and attended a couple of comedy shows that were quite entertaining, while encountering a most diversified crowd of people. One of the comedians had made it clear to the crowd that he was gay. He picked me out of the crowd, asking my name and where I was from. I felt I responded politely. Then he remarked that he had the feeling I would like to kick the crap out of him. I quipped back, "I don't know what you're into, but I don't think you can afford me." The crowd loved it.

When I left New York City, I drove down the coast, stopping at a few gun shops and leaving information about the Gilmore gun. All the time realizing that perhaps the rich and famous gun collectors were not in the places I could afford to go. While in New York, I had learned that eBay had sold its share of Butterfield and that the new partner was Bonham of England, now being called Bonham and Butterfield auctions. After a few days, I drove back to Baltimore, and flew home. What had been mentioned to me of the so-called prohibitive gun laws seemed worth investigating. So began the research of the government's requirements for relic or curio classifications.

Chapter Eight

The Government Weighs In

We've all heard the horror stories of trying to work with a government agency and how difficult it is. Well, it's nothing like you've heard; it's worse. Not always, of course; but if you ever feel a need for rejection and humiliation, just contact most any government agency. They will gladly meet your request—for a fee, that is.

I am not anti-government, and I do believe we have the best country and system on earth. But some government employees, particularly politicians, forget who pays their salary.

Here's how the trudge began for the saga of seeking a curio and relic (C&R) classification for the Gilmore Gun. To apply for the classification, I first called the Bureau of Alcohol, Tobacco, Firearms and Explosives known as the (ATF) and spoke with someone who naturally stated he was with the correct department for inquiries about curio and relic information. I explained to him what was needed; after a pleasant conversation, he gave me instructions and told me the pistol should easily qualify.

I asked how long it might take; he responded that it would be from six to eight weeks. After impatiently waiting three months, I called for an update. I soon learned the standard answer to any question posed to this department which is: "We get eight hundred to a thousand letters a year. What you want is not our main function. We will get to it when we can, but we can't say when." I heard this answer at least ten more times over the next two years.

Eight months passed with no response. I made more phone calls to the department. They passed me around from person to person and I heard the same responses over and over. When calling one day, I asked, "Who is the head of this department?" I was given his name. Of course he wasn't in, so I called back the next month, and the next. Each time I called, they said he wasn't there but would be back next week.

Finally one day I reached him, the chief of the department, and did have a very short chat. I told him about my classification request and asked when I might receive word about the request. He replied, "The longer I talk to you, the longer it will take." I couldn't help but bust out laughing and said, "Then it shouldn't take long, should it?" He didn't think my reply was funny. Not much more was said.

Another month passed and I made more calls. I asked for someone with more authority than the chief. The staffer on the line pleaded with me to "just give them a little more time." A week later I had my letter of denial. Needless to say, I was not happy.

This is the first letter I received from the BATFE.

DEPARTMENT OF THE TREASURY,
BUREAU OF ALCOHOL, TOBACCO,
AND FIREARMS
Washington, DC 20226
December 10, 2003

Dear Mr. Stilson:

This refers to your recent letter to the Bureau of Alcohol, Tobacco, Firearms, and Explosives (ATF). In your letter, you request that a Browning Challenger .22 caliber semiautomatic pistol that was used by Gary Gilmore to commit at least two cold-blooded murders be considered for classification as a curio or relic as that term is defined in the Gun Control Act (GCA) enforced by ATF.

An implementing GCA regulation, specifically, 27 Code of Federal Regulations (CFR), Part 478, s 478.11 (formerly Part 178/ s 178.11), defines curio or relic (C&R) firearms as those of which are of special interest to collectors by reason of some quality other than is associated with firearms intended for sporting use or as offensive or defensive weapons. To be recognized as curios or relics, firearms must fall within one of the following categories:

(a) Firearms which were manufactured at least 50 years prior to the current date, but not including replicas thereof; or

(b) Firearms which are certified to be C&R items of museum interest by the curator of a municipal, State, or Federal museum which exhibit firearms; or

(c) Any other firearms which derive a substantial part of their monetary value from the fact that they are novel, rare, bizarre, or because of their association with some historical figure, period, or event. Proof of qualification of a particular firearm under this category may be established by evidence of present value and evidence that like firearms are not available except as collector's items, or that the value of like firearms available in ordinary commercial channels is substantially less.

Our research indicates that the Challenger was introduced in 1962 and was produced in three variations (I, II, and III). Production ceased in 1985. Values for these pistols range from $110.00 to $1,450.00 (*Blue Book Gun of Values*, 24th edition). The Browning FN Challenger "Gold Line" and "Renaissance" engraved semiautomatic pistols were previously classified as "curios or relics."

With respect to the Browning Challenger model pistol in question, the murder of innocent victims by a deranged killer is not a sufficient and legitimate basis for granting it a C&R classification. This pistol does not derive a substantial part of its monetary value from the fact that it is novel, rare, bizarre, or because of its association with some historical figure, period, or event. Therefore, the Browning Challenger pistol in question does not merit consideration for classification as a curio or relic as defined in 27 CFR 478.11.

We thank you for your inquiry and trust that the foregoing information has been useful.

Sincerely yours,
Sterling Nixon
Chief, Firearms Technology Branch

After reading the qualifications for the curio and relic classification, I was totally bewildered. What looked obvious to me, but not Chief Nixon, was the part about the weapon deriving a substantial part of monetary value from the fact that it was rare and associated with a historical figure, period, or event.

I continued making calls to upper management of the BATF and received more empty promises. Finally, I received an informative and hopeful call from a fellow I had spoken with previously. He revealed to me, "We need a congressional response to look at this any further." I searched but didn't find that rule in the regulations. I think they were sure this revelation would sink me for good.

So I called the office of Chris Cannon, a Utah Congressman. After speaking with some wonderful and helpful people there, they extended an invitation to visit. This office and a few others were great to work with in spite of being government branches. My son and I went to the congressman's office and explained my request for a classification of the gun as a historical relic or curio. A few days passed and a call came from the Mr. Cannon's office. He had called Washington, DC and had someone call the BATF to see exactly what was needed in the "Congressional response." A letter was drafted and sent back to Utah then signed by the senator.

The letter read as follows.

CONGRESS OF THE UNITED STATES, HOUSE OF REPRESENTATIVES

Washington, DC 20515
January 16, 2004
James Zamillo

Bureau of Alcohol, Tobacco,
Firearms and Explosives
Office of Public and Governmental Affairs
650 Massachusetts Ave., NW, Room 8290

Dear Mr. Zamillo:

I am writing to support the request of Mr. Dennis Stilson to have a firearm classified as a Curio and Relic. I appreciate your attention to this matter.

It has been confirmed that the firearm for which the classification is being sought is the murder weapon used as evidence to convict Utah serial killer, Gary Gilmore. He became the first person to be executed after the U.S. Supreme Court allowed the reinstatement of the death penalty in 1976. This case, as you well know, was widely publicized and documented and was the subject of a best-selling novel and subsequent movie.

Under the most current standard, this item clearly has a value other than that of intended use as a sporting, offensive, or defensive weapon. The historic value of the .22 caliber Browning pistol is evident, and I believe that it merits official classification as a Curio and Relic. I appreciate your attention to this request. If you need any further information, please contact Megan Faulkner in my Provo Utah District Office.

Sincerely,
Chris Cannon
Member of Congress

I was very pleased to receive Chris Cannon's cooperation; not until after receiving his letter was there any mention of my hope to raise funds from the sale of this gun to open and operate a youth center. They were very pleased to hear my intentions and gave me information and links to apply for grants for funding. They also offered to help in any way they could.

I called for an appointment with the director of the Union Station Museum in Ogden, Utah. I hoped that another letter of qualification by the curator of a gun museum examining the weapon would strengthen my request and meet not only one but two of the qualifications. My father, my son, and I visited the museum a few days later, and it was quite an interesting place. This historical attraction includes the Utah State Railroad Museum, along with the John M. Browning Firearms Museum, which contains many prototypes of Browning guns and special editions.

The director examined the gun and wrote the following letter.

Ogden Union Station
James Zamillo
Bureau of Alcohol, Tobacco,
Firearms, and Explosives
Office of Public and Government Affairs
650 Massachusetts Ave., NW, Room 8290
Washington, DC 20226

Dear Mr. Zamillo:

On January 19, 2004 Mr. Dennis Stilson met with myself, at which time he let me examine a Browning Challenger serial #xxxxxxx. This gun appears to be unaltered, as did the serial number on the grip area. Mr. Stilson also presented documentation that demonstrates that this weapon, sadly, was used in a homicide in which Mr. Gary Gilmore was later found guilty of murder. The documentation was noted from the County Clerk and the evidence tag was still attached to the trigger guard.

Due to the landmark legal decisions that developed from this case, the gun has a character that is unique and unusual and would qualify as a Curio and Relic. The value of the gun due the unique circumstances that were aforementioned would be beyond the normal appraisal value of a weapon similar vintage and condition.

If you have any further questions please feel free to call me at the John M. Browning Firearms Museum at 801-629-8583.

Respectfully Yours,

Bob Geier
Executive Director
Browning Firearms Museum

It was now January. Armed with these two powerful letters, I felt I could not fail. I sent copies of both letters to the ATF. Finally, in May, a letter arrived from the ATF. I thought, "I've finally got it!" I ripped opened the letter—denied again. I've always been told, "Don't be a quitter."

Here is the letter from Chief Nixon.

U.S. Department of Justice,
Bureau of Alcohol, Tobacco,
Firearms and Explosives
May 19, 2004
Mr. Dennis R. Stilson
Spanish Fork, UT 84660

Dear Mr. Stilson:

This refers to your follow-up letter to the Firearms Technology Branch, ATF, which was received of February 2, 2004. Your reply concerned a Browning Challenger, .22 caliber semiautomatic pistol that was used by Gary Gilmore as a murder weapon, and our previous denial for classification as a "curio or relic" as that term is defined in 27 CFR S 478.11(formerly 178.11).

You have provided two letters of opinion favoring the classification of the Challenger pistol as a "curio or relic" (C&R) item as defined in 478.11. One letter was from Mr. Bob Geier, Executive Director, Browning Firearms Museum. The other letter was from Mr. Chris Cannon, Member of Congress, House of Representatives, 3rd District, Utah.

As you are aware, the above section provides that the term "curio or relic" is applicable to those firearms "which are of special interest to collectors by reason of some quality other than is associated with firearms intended for sporting use or as offensive or defensive weapons." To be recognized as curios or relics, firearms must fall within one of the following categories:

(a) Firearms which were manufactured at least 50 years prior to the current date, but not including replicas thereof; or

(b) Firearms which are certified to be C&R items of museum interest by the curator of a municipal, State, or Federal museum which exhibit firearms; or

(c) Any other firearms which derive a substantial part of their monetary value from the fact that they are novel, rare, bizarre, or because of their association with some historical figure, period, or event. Proof of qualification of a particular firearm under this category may be established by evidence of present value and evidence that like firearms are not available except as collector's items, or that the value of like firearms available in ordinary commercial channels is substantially less.

In order to meet the criteria for classification under subparagraph (b), it is imperative that the museum in which the curator is employed be a municipal, State, or Federal museum and not privately funded. Through our extensive research, we have reason to believe that Browning Firearms Museum is not a qualifying museum.

Also, with respect to the other cited criteria, the Challenger was introduced in 1962 and was produced in three variations (I, II, and III). Production ceased in 1985. Therefore, this firearm does not qualify as a curio or relic pursuant to subparagraph (a). Values for these pistols range between $110.00 and $1,450.00 (*Blue Book of Gun Values*, 24th ed.). As stated in our initial response to you, this pistol does not derive a substantial part of its monetary value from the fact that it is novel, rare, or bizarre, or from its association with an historical figure, period, or event. Therefore, this firearm does not qualify as a curio or relic pursuant to subparagraph (c).

We thank you for your reply and trust that the foregoing has been responsive.

Sincerely yours,
Sterling Nixon
Chief, Firearms Technology Branch

I was and still am confused as to the misinterpretation of phrases of the English language, such as "a substantial part of its monetary value" and so on. What am I missing here? In August, another letter arrived from Chief Nixon. It read identical to the preceding letter with the addition of one more paragraph, which stated as follows:

You are welcome to provide us with additional documentation regarding the status of the Browning Firearms Museum. If it can be demonstrated that this museum is a municipal, State, or Federal Museum, then the pistol would likely qualify for classification as a curio or relic. Please forward any relevant information to my attention.

We thank you for reply and trust that the foregoing has been responsive.

Sincerely yours,
Sterling Nixon
Chief, Firearms Technology Branch

I thought perhaps I had finally gotten somewhere but wondered, why the change of heart now? I called the Browning Museum again and found they were now changing to a private museum, which of course does not qualify. Thoughts of conspiracy raced through my mind. I telephoned the chief of the department with the BATF. This time he was polite and talkative and mentioned he had previously been to Utah and had spoken with both the museum and the Senator. The change of heart now made sense.

He finally admitted that the gun should qualify; but he said that he did not want to open a door for a new precedent. In his opinion, he revealed, the C&R classification would not benefit the sale, value, or legal ability to sell the gun anyway. He stated that with the documentation I already possessed from the FBI, no one could argue the Gilmore Gun's authenticity. I mentioned to him that after speaking with some California and New York residents, that I had a concern as to whether or not this pistol could be sold or bought without the C&R classification in these states.

He asked me to hold while he connected me with a "twenty-five year expert" and asked me to repeat my question and concern to the authority. So I repeated my question about the legal restrictions. This veteran expertly replied, "I'm not sure." That's certainly the reply of an expert, if I've ever heard one.

I gave up on trying for the C&R classification. I also learned that the Gilmore Gun is not illegal in the states I was concerned about.

I admit that I don't know all the BATF has to deal with on a daily basis. I must accept their decision. What else can I do? Obviously the pistol should have been awarded the Curio & Relic classification if they would only comply by the same rules they set.

Chapter Nine

Death to Killers:

The Public Speaks

In 2004, I was talking with a well known freelance reporter from California. I told her about the Gilmore Gun and she remembered the incident. She asked if I had heard of the Spitfire Grill story. I hadn't. It was a true story, later made into a movie, in which the owners of a restaurant held an essay contest awarding their restaurant as the prize.

I'm told that raffles are not legal unless you are a nonprofit organization. But by having an essay contest, the raffle is no longer chance, but skill. The story goes, to make a long story short, that they made a fortune, awarded the restaurant to the winner, and lived happily ever after.

I had heard about the owners of a bakery in Payson, Utah a nearby town who had recently tried the same thing, so I asked around and found the owners, talked with them, and put together my own essay contest. The bakery's contest failed, and I tried to learn from their experience. The owners said that first of all they should have set up a website and a merchant account which would provide the ability to accept credit cards.

Soon after, I visited the Spanish Fork city office one morning to speak with the mayor of Spanish Fork who at the time was Dale Barney. I was interested in his thoughts on the contest and his feelings about a community youth center in our city.

I told him the reason I wanted to promote this contest was to hopefully raise enough money to open, own, and operate a youth center. He was very supportive, and had previously considered a youth center for the city. But as always finding someone to run the program, and obtaining sufficient funds, presents a difficult task.

My essay contest was called "The UESSY" contest, the letters stood for nothing particular. To enter, the writer was required to compose an essay about his or her stand on the death penalty. Then submit the essay along with a hundred dollar entry fee. The judges of the contest would finalize four essays, finishing with two essays in favor of the death penalty, and two against.

The contestants would pick the winning essay of the final four. I thought it was a rare idea to let the contestants have the final vote. The prize was to be the Gilmore Gun, along with all the articles, authenticating documentation, etc.

I built a website, contacted attorneys, and searched the internet for legal rules and procedures. I stated in the rules that all funds would be returned if an insufficient amount of essays were entered. Also all essays became my property.

When launching the contest, I called the KSL television station in Salt Lake City and told them what I was doing. The woman I spoke with was honest and helpful. They were very interested and asked for the first interview.

I met with the interview crew the next day. This contest was during the presidential elections. This was bad timing on my part. The politicians were trying to steal my spotlight.

Again, the phones were ringing. The contest was front page on all the local newspapers and some surrounding state newspapers. And, of course, there were more television interviews. I'm not too shy, but at the time I did feel a bit nervous with this somewhat lengthy interview for television. I hoped to get enough exposure to receive five to ten thousand essays.

It was about this time that I received a call from a film producer in San Francisco. He expressed his interested in the contest and wanted to know more about it. He wanted to interview the judges, some of the people sending in essays, the previous owner, and me. His aim was to make a documentary-type film about the Gilmore gun and contest. He sent me a copy of a documentary he had done but I wasn't impressed.

The essays received were all interesting. Some of the essays were from people who had lost family and friends, and one from a close family friend with a story from his childhood we had never heard. Some were very emotional reading. I also talked with a number of the people further about their experiences.

Capital punishment is a difficult and controversial subject. Many of the essayists admitted that not until losing a loved one to murder, they became more in favor of the death penalty than before.

It is very hard to rationalize and justify killing another human, at least for most of us—until you have lost a loved one. That is why it is so difficult to confirm a belief without experiencing it.

The following are some of the essays received. I have quoted them just as they were written, with the exception of removing some of the names.

Essay Number One

Never before has a subject as the death penalty been the source of so much controversy and emotion. We humans are very passionate about our feelings about the death penalty.

I, for one, believe we have no right to take the life of another human being. Why, you ask? Because death alone scares the wits right out of us.

Death forces us to face emotions we would rather leave alone. Death is so final. If a person is executed and later found to be innocent, how do you bring that person back?

The right to choose the time of ones death is God's. No one else has the authority. One of God's commandments states, "Thou shalt not kill." Isn't that statement alone enough to stop executing people? I, for one, would not like to be left with the burden of choosing one's fate. Have those people who have chosen to live without any guilt?

I still see those out there who try and justify the death penalty. You say, well that person killed, so we will kill him or her because it costs so much money to house a prisoner these days. Execute them and be done with it.

I'm sure you've heard the one, they are not really dead, it's just the next step in an eternal journey, so let's execute them anyway.

We live in a society where human rights are so vital to our culture and to our right to survive. We proclaim to be civilized. Execution doesn't sound very civilized to me. We live in the twenty-first century, yet we still live in a wilderness.

Reading my view of the death penalty will cause some of you readers to hate me. Some of you will be disgusted. Some of you may agree with me.

Start up a conversation with someone and talk about the death penalty. Better yet, talk with someone who has the opposite view of the death penalty than you do. Watch and see how emotional they get. See how passionate they are toward their own feelings.

No, we do not have the right to take a life. It's time to change the laws and ban the death penalty forever. I believe we have the intelligence and technology to find other means of rehabilitation for those who are on death row now, and those who will land on death row in the future.

Come on people, this is America, the one country that has the real ability to accomplish the right thing.

Essay Number Two

The hangman's noose, electric chair, injection, or a bullet through the heart—they all spell death for the person on the receiving end.

Throughout the United States, injection is the common way to carry out the death sentence. However, the electric chair is still being used in some states, and not too long ago, it was the instrument of death in Utah.

Regardless of the method used, there is no guarantee of a quick death. Therefore, it becomes torture when a second attempt must be made after correcting what went wrong. It has happened many times in the past.

The death penalty extracts revenge for those associated with the victim, but falls short of a just punishment for the offender.

Life in prison without parole in my opinion would be a more appropriate punishment.

Then, there is the possibility that the accused may be innocent. Law enforcement and prosecutors sometimes exaggerate in order to obtain a guilty verdict. There are even cases on record where the investigator fabricated the evidence. The possibility also exists of a confused witness, or even more serious, a witness who out-and-out lies.

Since the introduction of DNA as evidence, many convicted people have been cleared and released from prison after serving many years for a crime they did not commit, reinforcing my belief that innocent people have been executed.

As part of my essay I am submitting a poem:

"Ode to the Electric Chair"
It waits there in silence, with no memory to forget,
For the footsteps in the hallway and the payment of a debt.
Guilty by the law, the chair did not decide.
When the warden pulled the switch, the person sitting in it died.

Now in perfect preservation stored with in those walls of gray,
The instrument of death awaits another time another day.
As it lounges in its glory we remember all too well,
The ending of its story when it sent those souls to hell.
The torment of their dying cannot escape those walls of gray,
Some indifferent and some crying on the eve of their last day.
Now dead their bodies be for sins tied to the past,
Their souls are not free and a ghostly image cast,
As silent footsteps walk the floor and faceless faces you cannot see,
The price they paid but pay no more. For a life of crime, was death to be.
When the moon casts shadows long and emotion fades with this dark night,
Write these words down in a song, two wrongs don't make a right.

Essay Number Three

In 1939, in my sixth year of age, I was exposed to a scene of the brutal and heinous murder of a dear old friend.

A little over a mile from our home at Lofgreen, Utah, lived a grey-headed, bearded gentleman by the name of Cadwell. He was a homesteader and lived alone in a cabin he built with his own two hands from cedar logs. He worked his land and had a one-man mining claim.

155

Sometimes, my dad and I would drive out to visit him to buy grain for our chickens and pass the time of day. Occasionally, we would walk out to his place hunting rabbits along the way. He would always come to the door to greet us.

One evening as we drove up to his spread, he didn't appear at the door as usual.

Dad said, "Something must be wrong, it's not like him to stay inside."

All was quiet.

We stopped the truck and Dad said, "You stay here, I will see what's wrong."

We could see the door was a little ajar. Dad called to the old man and pushed the door open. There on the floor in a pool of drying blood lay Mr. Caldwell. All around his body were spent pistol shells. He had been shot multiple times and the room had been ransacked.

We then drove to Eureka to notify the sheriff.

An intensive investigation ensued, much evidence was gathered.

It turned out that a well-known gang of local hooligans who thought the rumors were true that the old man had buried treasure on his place, had spent the night with him taunting and torturing him in an effort to lay their hands on the supposed treasure. When they couldn't find anything, they murdered him in cold blood.

Well, to bring conclusion to the story, may I say, the three who were responsible were quickly apprehended, were dealt with appropriately and faced the full extent of the law.

Since that awful day sixty-five years ago, I have known down deep in my heart that when anyone takes the life of another, he or she must pay the price with his or her own life.

Over the years, I have come to know that capital punishment is the only deterrent to bring stability to our society so that that law-abiding folks may feel safe. We must demand order in our fragile environment. The death penalty must be kept on the books and carried out in an expeditious manner for all guilty parties.

Essay Number Four

On June 3rd, 2003, our life was changed forever when our daughter was fatally shot three times by ———. He then wounded her boyfriend, —, when he finished firing the bullets in his gun. Then he called my former husband, ———, told him what he had done, and said he was on his way to his house to murder him, too.

The results of—'s murderous actions that morning made him eligible for the death penalty. We were requested to write a statement, as her parents, as to whether or not we could support the court in the sentencing of him to death.

This was an extremely difficult but a very necessary assignment. After much unrest within myself, I wrote the following statement, a 10/14/04 email titled "Death Penalty":

When it comes to the death penalty for ———, it is very hard on the family to ever think of him getting out of prison, and it is also very hard to think of the damage he could do while in prison with his threats toward us. We have suffered enough and will continue to suffer all of our lives because of his murderous actions. He has proven that to murder ———. He has proven that he cannot control himself. He has said that if he is ever free he will go after our family.

He has proven that he requires the full extent of the law to make sure he never harms or kills again. We deserve to be protected. We deserve to be safe and to have peace of mind. I don't want revenge; I just expect to be protected. He promised me that he would never hurt—in a conversation once when I begged him to leave her alone. He is a liar, a con, and a murderer. He thinks nothing of mind games and abuse. I don't believe that he can be rehabilitated. He tortured my daughter for months. He tortured all of us by torturing her. There is nothing they could legally do that would even come close to what he put my daughter through. I vote justice. The death penalty is easy compared to what he did. Let the judge decide. What would he want if it were his daughter? I am not God. I am just a mom who lost her daughter by his murderous hand. Just having to answer this feels horrible. It makes me feel sick inside.

Because the death penalty was in place, he took the plea of life without the possibility of parole.

As the case unfolded, the chances increased of a unanimous jury. He released himself of the chance of the death penalty. If the death penalty had not been in place, I doubt he would have pled. Who knows how lenient the court would have been, and who knows if our family would have received the protection we deserve.

Essay Number Five

Daniel Frank was put to death in 1622 in Virginia for the crime of theft. Since then the death penalty has been a feature of the criminal justice system, and it has come along way, baby. Despite what anti-death penalty supporters believe, the death penalty is the best extreme negotiating point to start with in capital murder cases.

You can only teach what you have experienced. The anti-death penalty supporters, the U.N., Amnesty International, etc., speak to abolish death penalties without personal experience. These words are balderdash. It becomes a trust issue.

- Can we trust the United Nations? No.
- Can we trust Amnesty International? No.
- Can we trust the Supreme Courts? Good question!
- Can we trust the Justice system? Sometimes.
- Can we trust the Prison system? I don't know.

What I can trust is my witness of the sadness, grief, and suffering at the loss of our daughter on June 30th, 2003, at the hands of ———.

Life without parole seems a small penalty to pay when applied to her killing. Without the death penalty, in the scheme of things, his sentence would have been lessened, his threats would still be alive, and society would be none the safer. The death penalty made sure that prison is the last sight he sees on earth.

Humans are like pendulums we swing from one extreme to the other. One lawyer argues death, the other argues life. We determine guilt or innocence, and after consideration of aggravating/mitigating circumstances we determine the sentencing-this or that.

The death penalty should be re-framed to mean something other than a deterrent to crime. It should remain the extreme in order to lead to the best alternative for the defendant, death or some form of life. An extreme of any other kind would result in lesser sentences and continued abuse of the justice system. I see no violation of human right or right to life laws for capital murderers. Should we allow the federal government to impose death penalty laws on all states? That would result in fairness, I'm sure. The best alternative, life without parole, does give some closure. However, crimes have been orchestrated within the prison walls. I personally heard a taped confession from (him)—threatening members of our family. Death would put a stop to that. Perhaps, because of the death penalty, he will see death in prison. Support for life without parole as the extreme would be great for the defendant and their family. I personally heard his mother say, "At least he won't die."

Having the death penalty allows for the law of mercy. One can complain about the cost of the death penalty, but I say the numbers can be crunched to support anyone's opinion. And the price of compassion is priceless. The death penalty statutes are not arbitrary or capricious, vague or ambiguous; they provide excellent guidance to jurors in deciding whether to apply the death penalty. The laws allow opportunity for the defendant to throw himself upon the mercy of the court and ask for compassion and prove their life to be worth saving.

It is my personal witness that without the death penalty being the extreme negotiating point in aggravated murder cases there would be lesser sentences than life without parole and our families would be in greater danger, our societies less safe, and the justice system would be more chaotic and more abused than it already is. Thanks to the death penalty, ——— and many other murderers will see prison as the last place on earth. For our safety, let's keep the death penalty alive. There will always be extremes, so let's not settle for anything less. God bless us all.

Chapter Ten

The Punishment of Death: Gilmore's Place in History

In Utah, where Gary Gilmore was put to death, there has always been a provision for execution, although the methods proposed have changed over time.

For example, in Utah State's earlier days Gary could have been beheaded, hanged, or shot by firing squad. No one actually was ever beheaded; and in 1888 the Utah law was changed to drop this method as an option. In 1980, hanging was eliminated as an available method, but lethal injection was added. So far, Utah has never executed a woman.

Utah allows the condemned to choose the method out of the available choices. Of course if the condemned refuses to choose, Utah makes the decision and in earlier days favored the firing squad. Today the state favors lethal injection.

To date, Utah has executed forty-seven criminals. Of these, thirty-nine were by firing squad, six by hanging, and two by lethal injection. The last criminal hanged was Barton

Kirkhamn in 1958. He had murdered two people in a Salt Lake City grocery store, and he selected hanging because it seemed to him that would put the state to the most trouble and inconvenience. The last Utah convict executed by firing squad, which was his method of choice, was John Albert Taylor on January 26, 1996. Prior to the death of Gary Gilmore who was executed for killing two young men in Utah County, who died by firing squad on January 17, 1977.

Utah first began using lethal injection when Pierre Dale Selby was put to death on August 28, 1987. He had murdered three people in Ogden's HiFi Shop thirteen years earlier, and he was only the second black man to be executed in Utah. Other minorities included two Hispanics and two Indians. All the others have been white men. Of the forty-seven executed men, twenty-five were non-Mormons and eight were Mormons. The religion of fourteen of the condemned could not be ascertained. The ages of those executed ranged from eighteen to sixty-four. The oldest was John D. Lee, put to death after being returned to the scene of the Mountain Meadows Massacre, twenty years after he'd committed the crime. Utah's condemned men sat on Death Row from eight days to thirteen years, the time from conviction to execution.

Utah's arranged two double executions. In 1854, two Ute Indians were executed together, by hanging, for killing two brothers in Cedar Valley. Seven years later on May 11, 1956 Verne Alfred Braasch and Melvin Leroy Sullivan were executed simultaneously by firing squad for the killing of a Beaver City gas station employee which occurred October 22, 1949.

Originally, executions in Utah usually took place in the counties where the crimes occurred and were carried out under the direction of the sheriff. In 1951, with the construction of the new prison at Point of the Mountain, executions were conducted at the prison. Firing squads were generally selected from volunteers among law enforcement officers of the county in which the crime occurred.

Among Utah's twenty-nine counties, thirteen have had crimes that resulted in executions. As could be expected, the more populous counties had more capital crimes, with Salt Lake County by far leading the way.

Compared to other states, Utah has always been considered rather unusual in that the condemned is given a choice as to the method of execution; only seven other states also provide more than one alternative. For example, Idaho and Oklahoma also provide firing squads as options. Those states that provide more than one method of execution as a general rule also allow the condemned to choose which method he or she prefers.

Utah's had several controversial executions. In 1878, Wallas Wilkerson was executed after his case became the first one heard "on appeal" by the U.S. Supreme Court, challenging execution as "cruel and unusual punishment." Joe Hill was executed on November 19, 1915 despite appeals of clemency from Helen Keller, President Woodrow Wilson, and the Swedish ambassador, which were ignored. In 1938, John Deering allowed his heartbeat to be monitored while he was being executed by firing squad.

On January 17, 1977, Gary Mark Gilmore became the first person executed in the United States after a nationwide moratorium on execution (all those under sentence of death had been released from Death Rows around the country ten years earlier). His execution renewed the capital punishment process that continues to this day. Under more strict guidelines from the Supreme Court, capital punishment laws and procedures were reinstituted and Death Rows in many states began again to fill.

In Utah, no one else was executed and no one joined the state's Death Row in 2001. Convicted killer Elroy Tillman came close; but he won a stay of his scheduled October 12, 2001 lethal injection.

The last man put to death in Utah was Joseph M. Parsons, who was executed by lethal injection in 1999 for murdering Richard L. Ernest from Loma Linda, California. Richard had made the mistake of giving Joseph a ride. Parsons is the sixth Death Row inmate to be executed in Utah since the U.S. Supreme Court reinstated the death penalty.

Execution through the Ages

The first established death penalty laws date back to the 18th century BC, in the code of King Hammaurabi of Babylon. The code prescribed the death penalty for twenty-five different crimes.

The death penalty was also part of other governments: the 14th century BC's Hittite code; the 7th century BC's Draconian code of Athens (which made death the only punishment for all crimes); and the 5th century BC's Roman law of the Twelve Tablets. Roman death sentences were carried out by such means as crucifixion, drowning, beating to death, burning alive, and impalement.

In the 10th century AD, hanging became the usual method of execution in Britain. In the following century, William the Conqueror would not allow persons to be hanged or otherwise executed for any crime, except in times of war.

This trend would not last; for in the 16th century, under the reign of Henry VIII, as many as 72,000 people are estimated to have been executed. Some common methods of execution at that time were boiling, burning at the stake, hanging, beheading, and drawing and quartering. Executions were carried out for such capital offenses as marrying a Jew, not confessing to a crime, and treason.

The number of capital crimes in Britain continued to rise throughout the next two centuries. By the 1700's, 222 crimes were punishable by death in Britain, including stealing, cutting down a tree, and robbing a rabbit warren. Because of the severity of the punishment of death, many juries would not convict defendants if the offense was not serious. This situation led to reforms of Britain's death penalty. From 1823 to 1837, the death penalty was eliminated for over 100 of the 222 crimes punishable by death.

The Death Penalty in America

Britain influenced America's use of the death penalty more than any other country. When European settlers came to the New World, they brought the practice of capital punishment. The first recorded execution in the new colonies was that of Captain George Kendall in the Jamestown colony of Virginia in 1608. Kendall was executed for being a spy for Spain. In 1612, Virginia Governor Sir Thomas Dale enacted the Divine, Moral, and Martial Laws, which provided the death penalty for even minor offenses such as stealing grapes, killing chickens, and trading with Indians. Laws regarding the death penalty varied from colony to colony. The

Massachusetts Bay Colony held its first execution in 1630, even though the Capital Laws of New England did not go into effect until years later. The New York Colony instituted the Duke's Laws of 1665. Under these laws, offenses such as striking one's mother or father, or denying the "true God" were punishable by death.

Early Questioning of the Death Penalty in Colonial Times

Those who did not support the death penalty found support in the writings of European theorists Montesquieu, Voltaire, and Bentham, and English Quakers John Bellers and John Howard.

However, it was Cesare Beccaria's 1767 essay, "On Crimes and Punishment," that had an especially strong impact throughout the world. In the essay, Beccaria theorized that there was no justification for the State's taking of a life. The essay gave abolitionists an authoritative voice and renewed energy, one result of which was the end of the death penalty in Austria and Tuscany.

American intellectuals as well were influenced by Beccaria. The first attempted reforms of the death penalty in the United States occurred when Thomas Jefferson introduced a bill to revise Virginia's death penalty laws. The bill proposed that capital punishment be used only for the crimes of murder and treason. Jefferson's bill was defeated by only one vote.

Dr. Benjamin Rush, a signer of the Declaration of Independence and founder of the Pennsylvania Prison

Society, challenged the belief that the death penalty served as a deterrent. In fact, Rush was an early believer in the "brutalization effect." He held that having a death penalty actually increased criminal conduct. Rush gained the support of Benjamin Franklin and Philadelphia Attorney General William Bradford. Bradford, who would later become the U.S. Attorney General, believed that the death penalty should be retained, but that it was not a deterrent to certain crimes. He subsequently led Pennsylvania to become the first state to consider degrees of murder based on culpability. In 1794, Pennsylvania repealed the death penalty for all offenses except first-degree murder.

19th Century Changes in the Death Penalty Laws

In the early part of the nineteenth century, many states reduced the number of their capital crimes and built penitentiaries. In 1834, Pennsylvania became the first state to move executions away from the public eye and carry them out in correctional facilities.

In 1846, Michigan became the first state to abolish the death penalty for all crimes except treason. Later, Rhode Island and Wisconsin abolished the death penalty for all crimes. Although some U.S. states began abolishing the death penalty, most states held on to capital punishment. Some states made more crimes capital offenses, especially for offenses committed by slaves. In 1838, in an effort to make the death penalty more palatable to the public, some states passed laws against mandatory death sentencing, instead enacting discretionary death penalty statutes. With the exception of a small number of rarely committed crimes in a few jurisdictions, all mandatory capital punishment laws had been abolished by 1963.

During the Civil War, opposition to the death penalty waned, as more attention was given to the anti-slavery movement. After the war, there emerged new developments in the means of executions. The electric chair was introduced at the end of the century. New York built the first electric chair in 1888; and in 1890, New York executed William Kemmler. Soon other states adopted this method of execution.

Execution in the Early and Mid-Twentieth Century

From 1907 to 1917, six states completely outlawed the death penalty, and three limited it to the rarely committed crimes of treason and first-degree murder of a law enforcement official. However, this reform was short-lived. There was a frenzied atmosphere in the country as citizens began to panic about the threat of revolution in the wake of the Russian Revolution. In addition, the nation had just entered World War I and there were intense class conflicts as socialists mounted the first serious challenge to capitalism. As a result, five of the six abolitionist states reinstated their death penalty by 1920.

In 1924, the use of cyanide gas was introduced, as Nevada sought a more humane way of executing its inmates. Gee Jon was the first person Nevada executed by lethal gas. The state tried to pump cyanide gas into Jon's cell while he slept, but this cell idea proved impossible, and the gas chamber was constructed.

From the 1920s to the 1940s, there was resurgence in the use of the death penalty. This resurgence was due in part to the writings of criminologists, who argued that the death penalty was a necessary social measure. In the United States, Americans were suffering through Prohibition and the Great Depression. There were more executions in the 1930s than in any other decade in American history, an average of 167 per year.

In the 1950s, public sentiment began to turn away from capital punishment. Many allied nations either abolished or limited the death penalty, and in the United States, the number of executions dropped dramatically. Whereas there were 1,289 executions in the 1940s, there were 715 in the 1950s; and the number fell even further, to only 191, from 1960 to 1976. In 1966, support for capital punishment reached an all-time low. A Gallup poll showed support for the death penalty at only 42%.

Constitutionality of the Death Penalty in America

The 1960s brought challenges to the fundamental legality of the death penalty. Before then, constitutional amendments such as the Fifth, Eighth, and Fourteenth were interpreted as permitting the death penalty. However, in the early 1960s, it was suggested that the death penalty was a "cruel and unusual" punishment and therefore unconstitutional under the Eighth Amendment. In 1958, the Supreme Court decided in *Trop v. Dulles*, 356 U.S. 86, that the interpretation of the Eighth Amendment contained an "evolving standard of decency that marked the progress of a maturing society." Although *Trop* was not a death penalty case, abolitionists applied the Court's logic to executions and maintained that the United States had, in fact, progressed to a point that its "standard of decency" should no longer tolerate the death penalty.

In the late 1960s, the Supreme Court began fine-tuning the way the death penalty was administered. To this effect, the Court heard two cases in 1968 dealing with the discretion given to the prosecutor and the jury in capital cases. The first case was *U.S. v. Jackson*, where the Supreme Court heard arguments regarding a provision of the federal kidnapping statute requiring that the death penalty be imposed only upon recommendation of a jury. The Court held that this practice was unconstitutional because it encouraged defendants to waive their right to a jury trial to ensure they would not receive a death sentence.

The other 1968 case was *Witherspoon v. Illinois*. The Supreme Court held that a potential juror's mere reservations about the death penalty were insufficient grounds to prevent that person from serving on the jury in a death penalty case. Jurors could be disqualified only if prosecutors could show that the juror's attitude toward capital punishment would prevent him or her from making an impartial decision about punishment.

Suspending the Death Penalty

The issue of the arbitrariness of the death penalty was brought before the Supreme Court in 1972 in *Furman v. Georgia* (408 U.S. 238). Furman had been robbing a home and accidentally shot the resident. Furman's lawyer, Anthony G. Amsterdam, bringing an Eighth Amendment challenge, argued that capital cases resulted in arbitrary and capricious sentencing. In nine separate opinions, and by a vote of 5 to 4, the Court held that Georgia's death penalty statute, which gave the jury complete sentencing discretion without any guidance on how to exercise that discretion, could result in arbitrary sentencing. The Court held that the scheme of punishment under the statute was therefore "cruel and unusual" and violated the Eighth Amendment. Thus, on June 29, 1972, the Supreme Court effectively voided 40 death penalty statutes, thereby commuting the sentences of 629 Death Row inmates around the country and suspending the death penalty because existing statutes were no longer valid.

Reinstating the Death Penalty

Although the separate opinions by Justices Brennan and Marshall stated that the death penalty itself was unconstitutional, the overall holding in Furman's case was that the specific death penalty statutes were unconstitutional. With that holding, the Court essentially opened the door to states to rewrite their death penalty statutes to eliminate the problems cited in *Furman*. Advocates of capital punishment began proposing new statutes that they believed would end arbitrariness in capital sentencing. The states were led by

Florida, which rewrote its death penalty statute only five months after *Furman*. Shortly after, thirty four other states proceeded to enact new death penalty statutes. To address the unconstitutionality of unguided jury discretion, some states removed all of that discretion by mandating capital punishment for those convicted of capital crimes.

However, this practice was held unconstitutional by the Supreme Court in *Woodson v. North Carolina*.

Other states sought to limit that discretion by providing sentencing guidelines for the judge and jury when deciding whether to impose death. The guidelines allowed for the judge and jury to consider aggravating and mitigating factors in determining sentencing. These guided-discretion statutes were approved in 1976 by the Supreme Court in such cases as *Gregg v. Georgia* (428 U.S. 153), *Jurek v. Texas* and *Proffitt v. Florida*. These cases are collectively referred to as the "*Gregg* Decision*.*" This landmark decision held that the new death penalty statutes in Florida, Georgia, and Texas were constitutional, thus reinstating the death penalty in those states. The Court also held that the death penalty itself was constitutional under the Eighth Amendment.

In addition to sentencing guidelines, three other procedural reforms were approved by the Court in the *Gregg* Decision. The first was bifurcated trials, in which there are separate deliberations for the guilt and penalty phases of the trial. Only after the jury has determined that the defendant is guilty of capital murder does it decide, in a second trial, whether the defendant should be sentenced to death or given the lesser sentence of prison time. Another reform was the practice of automatic appellate review of convictions and sentences. The final procedural reform from the *Gregg* Decision was proportionality review, a practice that helps the state to identify and eliminate sentencing disparities. Through this process, the state appellate court can compare the sentence in the case being reviewed with other cases within the state, to see if it is disproportionate.

Because these reforms were accepted by the Supreme Court, some states wishing to reinstate the death penalty included the reforms in their new death penalty statutes. The Court, however, did not require that each of the reforms be present in the new statutes. Therefore, some of the resulting new statutes include variations on the procedural reforms found in the *Gregg* Decision.

The ten-year moratorium on executions that had begun with the *Jackson* and *Witherspoon* decisions ended on January 17, 1977, with the execution of Gary Gilmore by firing squad in Utah. Gilmore did not challenge his death sentence. That same year, Oklahoma became the first state to adopt lethal injection as a means of execution. It would be five more years until a state tried the method; Charles Brooks became the first person executed by lethal injection in Texas, on December 2, 1982.

Limitations of the Death Penalty Within the United States

After World War II, many European countries abandoned or restricted the death penalty after signing and ratifying the Universal Declaration of Human Rights and subsequent human rights treaties. The United States retained the death penalty but established limitations on capital punishment.

In 1977, the U.S. Supreme Court held in *Coker v. Georgia* that the death penalty is an unconstitutional punishment for the rape of an adult woman if the victim was not killed. Other limits to the death penalty followed in the next decade.

Mental Illness, Retardation, and Execution

In 1986, the Supreme Court banned the execution of insane persons in *Ford v. Wainwright* (477 U.S. 399). However, in 1989, the Court held that executing persons with mental retardation was not a violation of the Eighth Amendment, *Penry v. Lynaugh*. Mental retardation would, instead, be a mitigating factor to be considered during sentencing.

Does Race Factor In?

Race became the focus of the criminal justice debate when the Supreme Court ruled in *Batson v. Kentucky* (476 U.S. 79) in 1977. The court ruled that a prosecutor who exercises his or her perogatory challenges to remove a disproportionate number of citizens of the same race in selecting a jury is required to show neutral reasons for the strikes. Race was again in the forefront when the Supreme Court decided the 1987 case *McCleskey v. Kemp*. McCleskey, who was black, had been convicted of murdering a policeman. His appeal alleged that Georgia's sentencing method discriminated against blacks. The appeal presented a statistical analysis showing a pattern of racial disparities in death sentences, based on the race of the victim. The Supreme Court held, however, that racial disparities would not be recognized as a constitutional violation of "equal protection of the law" unless intentional racial discrimination against the defendant could be shown. Thus McCleskey was put to death in 1991.

Can Juveniles Be Put to Death?

In the late 1980s, the Supreme Court decided three cases regarding the constitutionality of executing juvenile killers. In 1988, in *Thompson v. Oklahoma*, four Justices held that the execution of criminals aged fifteen and younger at the time of their crimes was unconstitutional. In this case, Thompson, a fifteen-year-old, had killed his brother-in-law, who had been abusing the teen's sister. The fifth vote was Justice O'Connor's concurrence, which restricted the ruling in Thompson to states without a specific minimum age limit in their death penalty statute. The combined effect of the opinions by the four Justices and Justice O'Connor in Thompson's case is that no state without a minimum age in its death penalty statute can execute someone who was under sixteen at the time of the crime.

The following year, the Supreme Court held that the Eighth Amendment does not prohibit the death penalty for crimes committed by juveniles at age sixteen or seventeen, *Stanford v. Kentucky* and *Wilkins v. Missouri*. At present, fifteen states bar the execution of anyone under eighteen at the time of his or her crime.

In 1992, the United States ratified the International Covenant on Civil and Political Rights. Article 6 (5) of this international human rights treaty requires that the death

177

penalty not be used on those who committed their crimes when they were below the age of eighteen. However, although the United States ratified the treaty, they reserved the right to execute juvenile offenders.

Does Innocence Count?

The Supreme Court addressed the constitutionality of executing someone who claimed innocence in *Herrera v. Collins* 1993. In this case, Herrara admitted to killing one police officer; but he claimed innocence in the death of another officer. Later, Herrara's brother claimed culpability for both murders. Although the Court left open the possibility that the Constitution bars the execution of someone who conclusively demonstrates that he or she is innocent, the Court noted that such cases would be very rare. The Court held that, in the absence of other constitutional violations, new evidence of innocence is no reason for federal courts to order a new trial. The Court also held that an innocent inmate could seek to prevent his execution through the clemency process, which, historically, has been the "fail safe" in our justice system. Herrera was not granted clemency, and he was executed in 1993.

Public Support of Execution

Clearly, public support for the death penalty has fluctuated throughout the century. According to Gallup surveys, in 1936, 61% of Americans favored the death penalty for persons convicted of murder. Support reached an all-time low of 42% in 1966. Throughout the 1970s and 1980s, the percentage of Americans in favor of the death penalty increased steadily, culminating in 80% approval in 1994. Since 1994, support for the death penalty has declined. Today, 66% of Americans support the death penalty. However, research shows that public support for the death penalty drops when poll respondents are given the two choices a juror in the penalty phase of a typical capital trial would be given: "death." or "life imprisonment with absolutely no possibility of parole." Given that choice, support for the death penalty drops to around 50%.

How Religions Regard the Death Penalty

In the 1970s, supporters of the death penalty included the National Association of Evangelicals (NAE), representing more then 10 million conservative Christians and forty-seven denominations, and the Moral Majority. NAE's successor, the Christian Coalition, also supports the death penalty. Today, Fundamentalist and Pentecostal churches, as well as the Church of Jesus Christ of Latter-day Saints (Mormons), support the death penalty typically on biblical grounds, specifically citing the Old Testament, (Bedau, 1997). A number of recent press reports regarding capital punishment in Utah have incorrectly implied that The Church of Jesus Christ of Latter-day Saints endorses the state's practice of using firing squads to carry out the death penalty.

Following is that Church's position on capital punishment:

"The Church of Jesus Christ of Latter-day Saints regards the question of whether and in what circumstances the state should impose capital punishment as a matter to be decided solely by the prescribed processes of civil law. We neither promote nor oppose capital punishment."

Although the Roman Catholic Church formerly supported capital punishment, that Church now opposes it. In addition, most Protestant denominations, including Baptists, Episcopalians, Lutherans, Methodists, Presbyterians, and the United Church of Christ, oppose the death penalty.

The Execution of Women

Women have, historically, not been subject to the death penalty at the same rates as men. Women have constituted only 3% of U.S. executions, from the first woman executed in the United States (Jane Champion, who was hanged in James City, Virginia in 1632) to the 1998 executions of Karla Faye Tucker in Texas and Judi Buenoano in Florida. In fact, only four women have been executed in the post-*Gregg* Decision era. In addition to Tucker and Buenoano, Velma Barfield was executed in North Carolina in 1984 and Betty Lou Beets was executed in Texas in February, 2000, (O'Shea, 1999, with updates by the Death Penalty Information Center).

Execution by the Feds

In addition to the states handing out the death sentence, the federal government has also employed the sentence for certain federal offenses, such as murder of a government official, kidnapping resulting in death, running of a large-scale drug enterprise, and treason. When the Supreme Court struck down state death penalty statutes in *Furman*, the federal death penalty statutes became softened in the same way that the state statutes did. As a result, death sentences under the old federal death penalty statutes have not been upheld.

A new federal death penalty statute was enacted in 1988 for murder in the course of a drug kingpin conspiracy. The statute was modeled on the post-*Gregg* Decision statutes that the Supreme Court has approved. Since its enactment, six people have been sentenced to death for violating this law, although no one has been executed yet.

In 1994, President Clinton signed into law the *Violent Crime Control and Law Enforcement Act*. This legislation expanded the federal death penalty to about 60 crimes—three of which do not involve murder. The three exceptions for which someone can be executed without committing a specific murder are espionage, treason, and drug trafficking in large amounts.

Two years later, in response to the bombing of the Murrah Federal Building in Oklahoma City, President Clinton signed more legislation in the same vein: the *Anti-Terrorism and Effective Death Penalty Act of 1996*. The building's destruction by Timothy McVeigh killed 168 people and injured hundreds of others, including children as young as two. The *Act*, which affects both state and federal prisoners, restricts review in federal courts by establishing tighter filing deadlines, limiting the opportunity for evidentiary hearings, and ordinarily allowing only a single habeas corpus filing in federal court. Proponents of the death penalty argue that this streamlining will speed up the death penalty process and significantly reduce its cost. On the other hand, some fear that quicker, more limited federal review may increase the risk of executing innocent defendants (Bohm, 1999 and Schabas, 1997).

How the Modern World Views Execution

In April 1999, the United Nations Human Rights Commission passed a resolution supporting a worldwide moratorium on executions. The resolution calls on those countries that have not abolished the death penalty to restrict its use, including not imposing it on juvenile offenders and limiting the number of offenses for which death can be imposed. Presently, more than half of countries have abolished the death penalty completely, *de facto*, or for ordinary crimes. However, over 90 countries retain the death penalty, including China, Iran, and the United States, all of which rank among the highest for executions in 1998.

Scorecard to Today's U.S. Executions

Execution by Year in the United States, 1930 to 2007

From the following table, it's very clear that the Gilmore case pivoted the country back towards capital punishment. Gary's execution was on January 17, 1977.

Number of Persons Executed in U. S.

1930	155	1940	124
1931	153	1941	123
1932	140	1942	147
1933	160	1943	131
1934	168	1944	120
1935	199	1945	117
1936	195	1946	131
1937	147	1947	153
1938	190	1948	119
1939	160	1949	119
1950	82	1978	0
1951	105	1979	2
1952	83	1980	0
1953	62	1981	1
1954	81	1982	2
1955	76	1983	5
1956	65	1984	21
1957	65	1985	18
1958	49	1986	18
1959	49	1987	25
1960	56	1988	11
1961	42	1989	16
1962	47	1990	23
1963	21	1991	14
1964	15	1992	31
1965	7	1993	38
1966	1	1994	31
1967	2	1995	56
1968	0	1996	45

1969	0		1997	74
1970	0		1998	68
1971	0		1999	98
1972	0		2000	85
1973	0		2001	66
1974	0		2002	71
1975	0		2003	65
1976	0		2004	59
1977	1		2005	60
			2006	53
			2007	42

States' Methods of Execution

State	Method
Alabama	Lethal injection or electrocution
Alaska	No death penalty
Arizona	Lethal injection or gas
Arkansas	Lethal injection or electrocution
California	Lethal injection or gas
Colorado	Lethal injection
Connecticut	Lethal injection
Delaware[3]	Lethal injection or hanging
District of Columbia	No death penalty

Florida	Lethal injection or electrocution
Georgia	Lethal injection
Hawaii	No death penalty
Idaho	Lethal injection or firing squad
Illinois	Lethal injection
Indiana	Lethal injection
Iowa	No death penalty
Kansas	Lethal injection
Kentucky	Lethal injection or electrocution
Louisiana	Lethal injection
Maine	No death penalty
Maryland	Lethal injection
Massachusetts	No death penalty
Michigan	No death penalty
Minnesota	No death penalty
Mississippi	Lethal injection
Missouri	Lethal injection or gas
Montana	Lethal injection
Nebraska	Electrocution
Nevada	Lethal injection
New Hampshire	Lethal injection or hanging
New Jersey	Lethal injection
New Mexico	Lethal injection

New York	Lethal injection
North Carolina	Lethal injection
North Dakota	No death penalty
Ohio	Lethal injection
Oklahoma	Lethal injection, electrocution, or firing squad
Oregon	Lethal injection
Pennsylvania	Lethal injection
Rhode Island	No death penalty
South Carolina	Lethal injection or electrocution
South Dakota	Lethal injection
Tennessee	Lethal injection or electrocution
Texas	Lethal injection
Utah	Lethal injection or firing squad
Vermont	No death penalty
Virginia	Lethal injection or electrocution
Washington	Lethal injection or hanging
West Virginia	No death penalty
Wisconsin	No death penalty
Wyoming	Lethal injection or gas
Federal system	Lethal injection
American Samoa	No death penalty
Guam	No death penalty

| Puerto Rico | No death penalty |
| Virgin Islands | No death penalty |

Table Footnotes:

1. Regarding Arizona, for those criminals sentenced after 11/15/92, only lethal injection is authorized.

2. Regarding Arkansas, for those convicts whose capital offense occurred on (or after) 7/4/83, only lethal injection is authorized.

3. Regarding Delaware, for those people whose capital offense occurred after 6/13/86, only lethal injection is authorized.

4. Regarding Kentucky, for those criminals sentenced on (or after) 3/31/98, only lethal injection is authorized.

5. Regarding New Hampshire, hanging is authorized only if lethal injection cannot be given.

6. Regarding Oklahoma, electrocution is authorized if lethal injection is ever held to be unconstitutional; and firing squad is authorized if both lethal injection and electrocution are held unconstitutional.

7. In Tennessee, for those convicts whose capital offense occurred after 12/31/98, only lethal injection is authorized.

8. In Wyoming, lethal gas is authorized if lethal injection is ever held to be unconstitutional.

9. In the federal system, for offenses under the Violent Crime Control and Law Enforcement Act of 1994, the method is that of the state in which the conviction took place.

10. Data's source: U.S. Bureau of Justice and the Death Penalty Information Center.

11. Note that as of March 1, 2005, the Supreme Court ruled that the Constitution bars capital punishment for crimes committed while the perpetrator is under age eighteen.

Crimes Punishable in the United States by the Death Penalty

Alabama—Intentional murder with 18 aggravating factors.

Arizona—First-degree murder accompanied by at least 1 of 10 aggravating factors.

Arkansas—Capital murder with a finding of at least 1 of 10 aggravating circumstances; treason.

California—First-degree murder with special circumstances; train wrecking; treason; perjury causing execution.

Colorado—First-degree murder with at least 1 of 17 aggravating factors; treason.

Connecticut—Capital felony with 8 forms of aggravated homicide.

Delaware—First-degree murder with aggravating circumstances.

Florida—First-degree murder; felony murder; capital drug trafficking; capital sexual battery.

Georgia—Murder; kidnapping (with bodily injury or ransom) when the victim dies; aircraft hijacking; treason.

Idaho—First-degree murder with aggravating factors; aggravated kidnapping.

Illinois—First-degree murder with 1 of 21 aggravating circumstances.

Indiana—Murder with 16 aggravating circumstances.

Kansas—Capital murder with 8 aggravating circumstances.

Kentucky—Murder with aggravating factors; kidnapping with aggravating factors.

Louisiana—First-degree murder; aggravated rape of a victim under age twelve; treason.

Maryland—First-degree murder, either premeditated or during the commission of a felony, provided that certain death eligibility requirements are satisfied.

Mississippi—Capital murder; aircraft piracy

Missouri—First-degree murder.

Montana—Capital murder with 1 of 9 aggravating circumstances. Capital sexual assault.

Nebraska—First-degree murder with a finding of at least one statutorily defined aggravating circumstance.

Nevada—First-degree murder with at least 1 of 14 aggravating circumstances.

New Hampshire—Six categories of capital murder.

New Jersey—Murder by one's own conduct, by, committed in furtherance of a narcotics conspiracy, or during the commission of the crime of terrorism.

New Mexico—First-degree murder with at least 1 of 7 statutorily defined aggravating circumstances.

New York—First-degree murder with 1 of 13 aggravating factors. Note that on June 24, 2004, the New York death penalty statute was ruled unconstitutional.

North Carolina—First-degree murder.

Ohio—Aggravated murder with at least 1 of 10 aggravating circumstances.

Oklahoma—First-degree murder in conjunction with a finding of at least 1 of 8 statutorily defined aggravating circumstances.

Oregon—Aggravated murder.

Pennsylvania—First-degree murder with 18 aggravating circumstances.

South Carolina—Murder with 1 of 10 aggravating circumstances.

South Dakota—First-degree murder with 1 of 10 aggravating circumstances; aggravated kidnapping.
Tennessee—First-degree murder with 1 of 15 aggravating circumstances.
Texas—Criminal homicide with 1 of 8 aggravating circumstances.
Utah—Aggravated murder.
Virginia—First-degree murder with 1 of 13 aggravating circumstances.
Washington—Aggravated first-degree murder.
Wyoming—First-degree murder.

Federal Laws Providing for the Death Penalty Homicide-related Crimes

Murder related to the smuggling of aliens.
Destruction of aircraft, motor vehicles, or related facilities resulting in death.
Murder committed during a drug-related drive-by shooting.
Murder committed at an airport serving international civil aviation.
Retaliatory murder of a member of the immediate family of law enforcement officials.
Civil rights offenses resulting in death.
Murder of a member of Congress, an important executive official, or a Supreme Court Justice.
Death resulting from offenses involving transportation of explosives, destruction of government property, or

destruction of property related to foreign or interstate commerce.

Murder committed by the use of a firearm during a crime of violence or a drug-trafficking crime.

Murder committed in a federal government facility.

Genocide.

First-degree murder.

Murder of a federal judge or law enforcement official.

Murder of a foreign official.

Murder by a federal prisoner

Murder of a U.S. national in a foreign country.

Murder by an escaped federal prisoner already sentenced to life imprisonment.

Murder of a state or local law enforcement official or other person aiding in a federal investigation; murder of a state correctional officer.

Murder during a kidnapping.

Murder during a hostage-taking.

Murder of a court officer or juror.

Murder with the intent of preventing testimony by a witness, victim, or informant.

Retaliatory murder of a witness, victim, or informant.

Mailing of injurious articles with intent to kill or resulting in death.

Assassination or kidnapping resulting in the death of the President or Vice President.

Murder for hire.

Murder involved in a racketeering offense.

Willful wrecking of a train resulting in death

Bank-robbery-related murder or kidnapping.

Murder related to a carjacking.

Murder related to rape or child molestation.

Murder related to sexual exploitation of children.
Murder committed during an offense against maritime navigation.
Murder committed during an offense against a maritime fixed platform.
Terrorist murder of a U.S. national in another country.
Murder by the use of a weapon of mass destruction.
Murder involving torture.
Murder related to a continuing criminal enterprise or related murder of a federal, state, or local law enforcement officer.
Death resulting from aircraft hijacking.

Non-homicide crimes that may result in a federal death sentence:

Espionage.
Treason.
Trafficking in large quantities of drugs.
Attempting, authorizing, or advising the killing of any officer, juror, or witness in cases involving a Continuing Criminal Enterprise, regardless of whether such killing actually occurs.

Chapter Eleven

International Headlines

On the evening of July 12, 2006 after completing the nightly ritual with my then eight year old son which included a mandatory three pin wrestling match, some reading and a prayer, he was off to sleep. Then, after slipping into my surfing attire, no boots required, I hit the waves of the web by diving into the seemingly endless sea of information searching for shimmering shells of information that might bring more light to this on-going story.

Tonight, for some reason or no reason, a murder auction site appeared on the screen and curiosity took control. Most of the items on this site consisted of artwork done by death row inmates and some documents that may have been signed before incarceration, etc. Not being a fan of these sites, I've spent little time reading them but must admit that I do believe those who choose to do so have their rights. Just because you or I may not participate in this type of collecting does not give us the right to reticule or judge others. You may like blue and I may prefer green but that is no reason to hate each other. You may feel more comfortable at a funeral than a wedding, I don't dislike you for that although I may not care to hang out and barbecue with you. I'm certain there are things we can agree on that can help us to tolerate each other in spite of our differences.

It was around midnight and with no particular hope or even a hint of expectation the Gilmore Gun was placed on a murder auction site with the beginning bid of one million dollars. It was nothing more than a whim with perhaps a touch of mischievous curiosity. Little did I know what might happen.

The next morning I left town for the night to escape the heat and went to the mountains for some serious hiking and cool fresh air.

The following afternoon, I returned to the valley and the ability of the cell phone to interrupt my life again. I had totally forgotten about the listing placed the night before.

The phone was filled with messages. The first three messages received were from the Salt Lake Tribune, the Salt Lake City Deseret News and the Associated Press which was followed by numerous others including acquaintances informing me of the breaking news story involving me. I returned some calls giving interviews to the Deseret News and the Associated Press but didn't have enough time to respond to any other messages which included requests for a response to some radio talk shows.

The tables had finally turned, bringing forth the opportunity to censure and bargain with the female reporter of the Associated Press telling her of my disappointment and concerns of the slant and the untruthful quotes used in the last interview I had granted. After receiving her humble apologies and promises of a more factual interview, I conceded. Debbie Hummel did the interview for Associated

Press article while being reasonably polite throughout the conversation.

The interrogation began with the eminent question "Did you place the Gilmore Gun on this auction?" I answered "yes" but no one ever asked if I still owned the pistol. This was followed by various other questions all the while building up to the significant question asking if I was aware of the Utah State law that had been passed in 2004 which is as follows-

78-61-101. Definitions.

As was in this chapter:

(1) "Conviction" means an adjudication by a federal or state court resulting from a trial or plea, including a plea of no contest, nolo contendere, a finding of not guilty due to insanity, or not guilty but mentally ill regardless of whether the sentence was imposed or suspended.

(2) "Fund" means the Crime Victim Reparation Fund created in Section 63-63a-4.

(3) "Memorabilia" means any tangible property of a person convicted of a first degree or capital felony, the value of which is enhanced by the notoriety gained from the conviction.

(4) "Profit" means any income or benefit over and above the fair market value of the property that is received upon the sale or transfer of memorabilia.

Enacted by Chapter 368, 2004 General Session
78-61-102. Profit from sale of memorabilia -- Deposit in Crime Victim Reparation Fund -- Penalty.

(1) Any person who receives a profit from the sale or transfer of memorabilia shall remit to the fund:
  (a) a complete, itemized accounting of the transaction, including:
    (i) a description of each item sold;
    (ii) the amount received for each item;
    (iii) the estimated fair market value of each item; and
    (iv) the name and address of the purchaser of each item; and
  (b) a check or money order for the amount of the profit, which shall be the difference between the amount received for the item and the estimated fair market value of the item.
(2) Any person who willfully violates Subsection (1) may be assessed a civil penalty of up to $1,000 per item sold or transferred or three times the amount of the unremitted profit, whichever is greater.

Enacted by Chapter 368, 2004 General Session

I can clearly see the concern of some for this type of law but they are forgetting the big picture. What ever happened to free enterprise? These types of narrow-minded self-serving agendas are what destroy the Constitution and our freedom. This law has been found unconstitutional in all but five states and rightfully so.

I had heard of the "Son of Sam Law" which seems reasonable and proper to me. Naturally I had no intentions of breaking any laws but was confused because others had referred to the prior law above as the "Son of Sam Law." Being somewhat familiar with this law, I was perplexed as to how it could relate to me.

In the article, an assistant to the Attorney General was quoted as saying "if the gun is sold, we will confiscate the money." Here is the quote from the article.

"The Utah Attorney General's Office on Wednesday suggested the sale of Gilmore Gun may violate its so-called "Son of Sam" law passed in 2004." This is where the confusion began because this was not the "Son of Sam Law." The media and perhaps the government employees were both confused and had made a mistake. The article continued by saying "It comes under the definition of memorabilia," Assistant Utah Attorney General Sharel Reber said in the article, "What we're looking at is the sale."

"It appears he's on notice about the law," said Cheryl Luke with the Utah Department of Public Safety and the attorney who would likely file any case for the crime victim's fund.

"Luke said she would not file anything official unless the gun is sold for well over its fair market value." *Associated Press* July 13, 2006.

The *Associated Press* article began by stating that the gun used by Gary Gilmore to commit his crimes is being offered on an auction site with a beginning bid of one million dollars. The commentary proceeded with primarily the repeat of some facts such as the case that ended the ten year period of no executions in America, the prior books and movies and my hopes to make something good from my personal association with this case.

A few days later I continued to become more and more agitated with what the media had misrepresented. While hoping for some explanations created by the media, I pulled on my Cordovan colored snakeskin boots with the dark brown tops with stitching to match, and then, with the article in hand, traveled to the Salt Lake City Capital and visited the Attorney General's office looking for answers. He was not available, what a surprise, I asked for the person who had made the comment in the article, Sheryl Reber, an assistant to the Attorney General. Her office was not at the Capital Building but downtown Salt Lake City at the Heber Wells building.

When she first appeared, I introduced myself and asked about the law concerning the sale of items related to capital crimes. She looked puzzled for a moment then replied "You're the guy with the gun." Sheryl struck me as an attractive woman with an intelligent and aware presence. She was also very helpful and polite; not what I expected. I expressed my concerns then inquired if perhaps I could read the law. She asked me to please wait while she retrieved the state law manual.

After reading the law, which coincidently was the last entered into this thick state book of laws, I responded truthfully saying that I was unaware of such a law and would, of course, comply. She seemed empathetic and said she was sorry that this was the law but it was the law. I appreciate her taking the time to explain so courteously and her kind response. Feeling somewhat satisfied, I drove home.

Next, I searched out the Utah version of the Son of Sam Law and it is as follows:

Citation: UTAH CODE ANN. art. 77-18-8.3 (2000)
History: Enacted in 1996 to replace 78-11-12.5 (enacted 1991 and repealed in 1996).

TITLE 77. UTAH CODE OF CRIMINAL PROCEDURE
CHAPTER 18. THE JUDGMENT
Utah Code Ann. 77-18-8.3 (2000)
77-18-8.3. Special condition of sentence during incarceration -- Penalty

(1) At the time of sentence, the court may order the defendant to be prohibited from directly or indirectly engaging in any profit or benefit generating activity relating to the publication of facts or circumstances pertaining to the defendant's involvement in the criminal act for which the defendant is convicted.

(2) The court's order may prohibit the defendant from contracting with any person, firm, corporation, partnership, association, or other legal entity with respect to the commission and re-enactment of the defendant's criminal conduct, by way of a movie, book, magazine article, tape recording, phonograph record, radio, or television presentations, live entertainment of any kind, or from the expression of the defendant's thoughts, feelings, opinions, or emotions regarding the criminal conduct.

(3) The court may order that the prohibition includes any event undertaken and experienced by the defendant while avoiding apprehension from the authorities or while facing criminal charges.

This particular law makes complete sense to me. No defendant or his family should ever have the opportunity to profit from their crime.

The article telling of the million dollar auction appeared for the next three days in most of the newspapers in North America and Canada, some in Europe along with television and many other media internet sites. Most of the stories were similar quoting the Associated Press article. Some of the headlines varied such as "Gilmore Gun goes on sale for $1 Million" or "Gun Purportedly Used by Gilmore Auctioned" and "Gary Gilmore's gun available on murder auction site." One of my favorite opening statements was listed by David Usborne in *New York Published* July 15, 2006 which stated "Scholars and supporters of capital punishment in the United States are being given the chance to purchase at auction what may be the rarest of all death-penalty souvenirs - the handgun purportedly used by Gary Gilmore to murder a motel clerk in Utah almost 30 years ago."

Again, the position is in the eye of the beholder whether right or wrong, good or bad, or which team you are on. Few historical events are free of some tragic elements otherwise why would we remember them. Events such as wars, assassinations, riots; it all depends on your stand as to what is correct.

I find it interesting, although unfair, how the more liberal slant seems to take precedence in most stories that do reach the mainstream media and often a failure to confirm facts, or ignore them. At least the woman who interviewed me for the *Associated Press* asked if I had anything I would like to add to the story and also assured me that I could approve what was written before releasing the interview. Although I didn't bother with the offer to prescreen the article she did get most of the facts correct.

Chapter Twelve

Should Gilmore Have Been Executed?

This chapter begins with a theory by a Richard Salazar Ph. D. who has obviously given much thought to the subject of the rationale for executions such as Gary Gilmore's.

The Legal, Moral, and Religious Basis for Capital Punishment

Why Execution is legally Right

Arguments supporting the legal basis for the death penalty will be developed by examining the Constitution and the Bill of Rights. Before this examination is undertaken, let us recall what happened in 1787-1789. Thirteen states (that is, the people, speaking through their duly elected representatives of the people) came together and formed a federal system of government by ratifying the then newly drafted Constitution. This action created the federal government. Consequently, the federal government is an offspring of state action. The states came first. The preamble to the Constitution makes it clear the federal government is to serve the people, that is, the states. The Constitution was created to provide a federal government with sufficient authority to discharge its obligation to serve the people.

There are those who propose that since the states created the federal government, the states ought to be sovereign. This seems to suggest when push comes to shove on questions involving the authority to act on issues not mentioned in the Constitution, the states win. Others point out the Civil War made it clear the federal government was sovereign; consequently the states ought to give way. Perhaps the truth of the matter is that both are equally sovereign; in fact, share conjoined sovereignty.

After ratification of the constitution, a convention was called to address the felt need for listing the rights of the people within the newly created government. Some states ratified the proposed Constitution on condition such a convention would be held. The first ten amendments to the Constitution, the Bill of Rights, was the product of that convention.

The motivation behind itemizing the Bill of Rights was a fear the newly created federal government would usurp authority and exercise excessive authority, a fear growing out of the colonial experience in dealing with some of the governors during the colonial period. This fear also grew out of a clear understanding that the passions and principled use of authority can lead to unprincipled use of authority—in short, tyranny in one form or another. Those favoring the Bill of Rights were not content with the implied limitation of federal powers in the Constitution. Their intent was to make the limitations of federal powers explicit.

There were some who were uneasy with the idea of itemizing a Bill of Rights. Their uneasiness grew out of a fear some important right might not be listed and therefore assumed not to exist. Owning and having control over property, real estate, seems to be one such right. Being able to disagree with the dominant political or social thought of the community without a risk of legal or social penalties for such thoughts is another such right.

The first nine of the rights listed in the Bill of Rights itemize specific rights of the people that the federal government cannot violate. The Tenth is a blanket statement limiting federal authority. The Tenth Amendment makes it clear any governmental power not granted the federal branch by the Constitution and not denied the states by the Constitution, was denied the federal government and reserved for the states. One such power is the power to redistribute wealth. Redistributing wealth entails collecting wealth through taxation, and then dispensing the wealth through various government agencies. High-sounding reasons are always proposed to justify this government action; but the fact remains that redistribution of wealth, a form of plundering the wealth of the people, in all its forms, is unconstitutional.

The Constitution, in Article One; Section nine, declares no bill of attainder shall be passed. This is a restriction upon the federal government. In Section Ten of Article One, the Constitution applies the same restriction to the states. A bill is a proposed law. Attainder means a person is deprived of all civil rights and capacities because the sentence of death has been passed upon that individual. The restriction on bill of attainder means that people who have had the penalty of death passed upon them cannot be deprived of all rights. For example, these individuals have at least the right to be fed, clothed, and housed while awaiting execution.

In Article Three of the Constitution we read "The Congress shall have power to declare the punishment of treason, but no attainder of treason shall work corruption of blood, or forfeiture except during the life of the person attained." The phrase "corruption of blood" grew out of the practice of punishing not only the treasonous individual, but also the family and descendants. The word "forfeiture" means the property of the guilty party and of the family, and their descendants, was subject to being seized by the government. Such was the practice in those days. The Constitution limited that practice such that it could be applied only so long as the condemned individual lived. This provision of the Constitution has worked very well, perhaps even better than anticipated. There is no "corruption of blood" or "forfeiture" in our society.

The Bill of Rights specifies additional legal rights for those who are charged with a capital offense. The Fifth Amendment protects individuals from double jeopardy and self-incrimination and requires the federal government to employ due process of law before depriving anyone of life. The Eighth Amendment prohibits cruel and unusual punishment. Thus, the condemned individual cannot be tortured in any way. The Fourteenth Amendment requires states to employ due process of law before an individual can be condemned to death for a capital offense.

Due process of law requires a government to take certain steps before imposing a capital penalty prescribed by law. Some such steps, in addition to the Eighth and Fourteenth Amendments, include a grand jury indictment, a trial by a jury of one's peers, adherence to the rules of evidence, assumption of innocence until proven guilty, and proof of guilt beyond reasonable doubt. There is to be no rush to judgment in applying capital punishment. This concern for due process in capital offenses does not mean the Constitution prohibits capital punishment.

The fact that cruel and unusual punishment and capital punishment are mentioned in separate amendments means the writers of the Bill of Rights (many of them were also writers of the Constitution) recognized a distinction between the two. Consequently, capital punishment, in and of itself, did not constitute cruel and unusual punishment to those men who hammered out the Constitution and the Bill of Rights. The recognized death penalty in that day was by hanging. Therefore, hanging was not considered cruel and unusual by those who wrote the Constitution.

The Constitution is silent on the question of the age of those on whom the death penalty is imposed. The Constitution makes no statement about a person being too young or too old for the death penalty. The Supreme Court ruled in March 2005 that the death penalty for those who were under the age of eighteen when they committed a capital offense was unconstitutional.

If the word "unconstitutional" means there are statements in the Constitution which specifically prohibits the death penalty for those under age 18. The Supreme Court decision is correct. And if there are no such statements in the Constitution the Supreme Court decision misrepresents the

Constitution. The fact of the matter is the Supreme Court is silent on the question of age limitation in cases of capital offenses.

The Supreme Court has two choices. One would be to refuse to hear the case. The other is to send the question to Congress asking them to initiate the amendment process. In the first option the Court is saying the challenge to some current practice or law does not have standing; that is, the case has no merit. In the second choice, the Court is saying an issue needs to be addressed, which in turn requires an amendment to the Constitution. Provisions for amendments make the Constitution a living and breathing document by possessing flexibility to adapt to different situations not foreseen by the Founders; And does so by requiring the consent of the people in each of the states.

The fact that the Supreme Court set age limits on the death penalty where the Constitution had none means the Constitution has in effect been amended by judicial decree; a de facto amendment. This means the amendment process as specified in the Constitution has been circumvented. This applies to Court decisions on school prayer, abortion, school integration, and requiring both houses of state legislatures to be elected on the basis of population. Previously the states with bicameral legislatures had followed the pattern of the federal government, where one chamber was elected on a geographic basis and the other on a population basis. The disturbing fact about de facto amendments is that the people have no voice in the amendment process.

De facto amendments open the door to political mischief. When a de facto amendment to the Constitution is permitted, what is to prevent a second de facto amendment, a third, and on and on, until the Constitution becomes so cluttered it is no longer recognizable? Nothing. De facto amendments create conditions where only a few people can exert their will without consulting the will of the people, violating the principle of consent of the governed. So much for the Bill of Rights and for the preamble of the Constitution which proclaims the Constitution is for the people.

The recent incorrect Supreme Court decision regarding an age limit for capital punishment grows out of the erroneous belief the Supreme Court is to interpret the Constitution. This belief presupposes the Court will determine the intent of the Constitution, which presupposition invites de facto changes in the Constitution.

Determining the intent of the Constitution can only be accomplished by examining the intent of those who authored the Constitution. This requires well-grounded knowledge of the history of that period of American history and a consulting of the written record left behind by the men involved. Those who authored the Constitution know best what they intended.

This approach should also be applied to enforcing laws. This should be a legal precedent. The founders of this country accepted the death penalty, and so should we.

Some might complain the practice of being guided by the thinking of those who wrote the Constitution is the same as being guided by men long since dead, claiming such is not wise. If such doctrine is accepted, then let us throw out the idea men are equal in the law. That notion is found in the Declaration of Independence, which predates the Constitution.

This brief review clearly demonstrates the legal justification for the death penalty.

The moral basis for the death penalty grows out of the definition of the word "moral." In this effort, only the dictionary will be used. This will prevent a babble of multiplied definition, in which babble hinders understanding. Moral is defined as having a concern for the right and the wrong of things.

In any community, there is moral position held by the majority on any given topic. In a republic such as the United States, where representatives of the people legislate law, debate by the representatives reflects the moral position of the majority. Only those moral positions which have support of the majority become law. A law which emerges from this process reflects the moral values, i.e., what is felt to be right and what is wrong, by the majority of the people.

Clearly then, laws are a moral force in a community, a moral force approved of by the majority.

The question of force arises when the issue of enforcing the law is considered. Those who break laws do not routinely walk into the courthouse and admit they broke law X and hand over money to cover the fine for that particular violation. Nor do any of them volunteer to be jailed for crime X.

Police have to chase criminal. Criminals are restrained by jails, handcuffs, leg shackles, strait jackets, and jails. When the legal process determines guilt, force is required in enforcing the provisions of the law. One concludes coercion can be applied when the law is enforced. However, the coercion is applied after the fact, not before the fact.

Law also has an educative function. In any community, if the behavior X has been identified as illegal that means behavior X is considered wrong by that community. There are some individuals who are not raised with a clear sense of right or wrong. By looking to the community, which includes its legal structure, these individuals can determine what is right or wrong in that community; hence the educative function of the law. And it seems the more serious the crime, the more important the educative function.

If an individual commits crime X and goes unpunished or perhaps even seemingly rewarded a message is communicated is that in the case of crime X, there are no negative legal consequences. This will encourage others to do the same. Consequently, in a community, crime tends to do evil in that community. The negative educative function of the law, in situations such as these, is not good for society. Punishing criminals helps to retain the moral value of the community. Therefore, if society wishes to survive, it has a vested interest in seeing to it that criminals are punished. Virile societies punish criminals. It is the degenerate, morally corrupt society that whitewashes and does not punish the criminal.

Before proceeding, let us recall that there is to be no rush to judgment in the use of the death penalty. Circumstantial evidence alone, it seems, is not enough to warrant such a penalty. There has to be no doubt the accused committed the murder. A period of time for the defense to file a motion to review the evidence seems to be a necessary precaution in all cases.

There are those who argue against capital punishment by pointing out putting a murderer to death will not bring back to life the victim(s) who died at the hands of the murderer. Neither will failure to apply the death penalty. Obviously then, the question of whether the murdered victim can or cannot be brought back to life by any action or inaction of the community is totally beside the point.

There are those who claim they value human life so highly they are adamantly against capital punishment for any reason. If life is of such a high value, what about those who deny life to others when they commit murder? Shouldn't there be a severe penalty for violating one of the highest, if not the highest value of society? Don't murderers forfeit their right to life because of what they have done? Allowing murderers to live makes a mockery of the claimed high value of human life, particularly to the murdered. Or, is society saying, once a person is dead, that life, in totality, including memory of that life, is of little value? In any situation where the murderers live, means the murderer has more merit than his victim(s); after all, the murderer is alive and the victim(s) is (are) not.

There are those who support the death penalty when the murder is particularly gruesome or violent. These crimes are often described as "heinous" and argue a heinous murderer deserves to be put to death. But, isn't the taking of life of any human being a heinous act? All murderers ought to be punished by a penalty that fits their crime.

The appropriateness of prolonged prison terms for capital offenses as an alternative to the death penalty seems questionable. When society does not exercise capital punishment for murderers and opts for the less severe penalty of long prison sentences, society has to bear the high cost of such. This means society is also being punished. This does not seem proper.

There are those who claim application of the death penalty is ineffective, that it does not deter crime. No rational human being can appropriately make such a definitive statement because there is no scientific evidence to support such a statement. True, there are articles in the journals of sociology, psychology, and criminology which claim the death penalty has no deterrent effect. Some journals even claim capital punishment is associated with higher rates of murder. However interesting these articles may be, we should keep in mind these articles do not reflect science. These articles are usually based on surveys, and surveys are not science.

Science calls for the scientific method. The scientific method requires testing of ideas (theories) with experiments. There are simply no experiments with capital punishment to see if such deters crimes.

The experiments, in order to determine deterrence (or lack thereof) of capital punishment for murder, would need to take place in several stages. The first would be to measure the effect of executing a small percent, say two percent, of all murderers across wide regions of the country over a span of several years. The findings would be compared to wide regions of the country similar in makeup, where there is no capital punishment. If the findings show no deterrent effect of the death penalty, that means a two percent application of the penalty does not deter. The deterrent effect, or lack thereof, of the death penalty is still an open question.

A second stage of the experiment, using the concept of a control and experimental group, would require, say five percent of all murderers to receive capital punishment. Again, this second stage would be carried out for a number of years. Stage three might require ten percent of all murderers, stage four fifteen or twenty percent, stage five calling for thirty percent, stage six demanding forty percent, and so on. Such a study might reveal if the certainty of facing death at the hands of the government might be the deterrent factor, not the percentage of murderers put to death. Such a phenomenon is similar to speed traps on the highways. It is the high certainty of being caught and punished that deters. And if there is a deterrent effect of law enforcement in capital cases then society benefits.

Only after an experiment such as this could anyone have any certainty that the death penalty does or does not deter murder. Because no such studies have been conducted, at present, no rational being can say with scientific certainty that application of the death has no deterrent effect or that it increases the murder rate.

Such a prolonged experiment as suggested requires that if we are to attempt to be scientific about the question. Perhaps discover that even if carried to the extreme where one hundred percent of the murderers were executed, if capital punishment would fail to deter murders. There seems to a segment of the population who are determined to do what they wish regardless of what the penalties are. To these, no punishment of others deters them. A finding such as this should not be the basis of concluding capital punishment should be done away with. Such a decision would be to use the lowest common denominator of the population to determine legal and moral standards for the rest of the population. Such an approach would be like using a cesspool as a standard to determine safe clean drinking water.

The question of deterrence may be beside the point. Because society has a vested interest in preserving itself, is not punishment of the murderers the primary concern for society?

Since laws reflect the moral values of the majority, it seems clear there is a moral case for the death penalty.

The King James Version of the Bible will be the basis for examining the religious position on the subject of capital punishment.

This discussion will focus on what is known as "an eye for an eye and a tooth for a tooth." Most Christians recognize the practice of exacting an eye for an eye and a tooth for a tooth as punishment as part of the Law of Moses. The Law of Moses also included other teachings, rituals, and offerings as taught by Moses.

Christian scholars are in agreement that with the death of Jesus Christ the Law of Moses was fulfilled, that is, the law had been done away with-it was no longer in effect.

Many Christians believe capital punishment was part of "an eye for an eye and a tooth for a tooth." These would argue that the fulfilling of the Law of Moses does away with capital punishment.

But, this belief is misplaced. The practice of capital punishment was introduced in the days of Noah, as recorded in Genesis 9:6 which reads "Whoso sheddeth man's blood, by man shall his blood be shed: for in the image of God made he man."

Scriptures from the Old Testament will now be reviewed to more completely explain the Christian position on the death penalty.

In Exodus, Chapter 21, Verse 12, we read "He that smiteth a man, so that he die, shall be surely put to death," and in Verse 14, "But if a man come presumptuously upon his neighbour to slay him with guile; thou shalt take him from my altar, that he may die." Verses 15, 16, and 17 provide for the death penalty for striking one's parents, for stealing a man (kidnapping) and for cursing one's parents. Verses 22 and 24 deal with the case where there is injury to a pregnant woman such that she has a miscarriage. Verse 22 specifies a penalty, "according as the woman's husband will lay upon him…" to which a fine is added. And, if "mischief follows" the miscarriage, Verses 23 and 24 specify the penalty matches the mischief inflicted on the woman, including an eye for an eye, wound for wound, even life for life.

Genesis 21:28-29 deal with cases where an ox gored an individual with a fatal outcome. If the owner is told his ox gores people, and the ox is not restrained, and the ox gores another to death, both the ox and owner are put to death.

This brings to mind the case of the two lawyers in San Francisco whose pit bulls killed a female tenant. Their pit bulls were not restrained even after the owners were warned of the viciousness of their dogs. One wonders what the educative effect would have been if the lawyers had also been put to death.

Leviticus 24:17-21 clearly points out if a person kills someone, then that person shall surely be put to death.

In Numbers 35:11-15, 22-29, Moses established six cities of refuge for those who accidentally kill another person; in addition, Moses is said to have provided the death penalty for those who killed by using weapon of iron or wood, or by throwing a stone (sling shot?), stabbing, or hitting with the hands. Congregations decided in cases of accidental death, and sent the person who accidentally killed to one of the six cities of refuge. A high priest from the same congregation was appointed, and so long as the appointed high priest lived, the city of refuge remained safe for the party who accidentally killed. If this party was found outside of refuge while the appointed high priest lived, she or he was subject to death if found by a person called "avenger of blood" outside a city of refuge. Once the appointed high priest died, the person who accidentally killed could safely return to his or her own city. Joshua 20:1-6 says the same thing with one additional provision. The man fleeing to a city of refuge is to state his reason for entering city to the city officials, presumably so the officials could arrange for protection.

Numbers 11:16-21 specify different cases murder, i.e., if the killing is with a stone, an "instrument of iron," or by hand, the murderer shall be put to death. The "avenger of blood" can kill this person on sight.

It appears the "avenger of blood" is some sort of bounty hunter. Clearly the "avenger of blood" needs to be kept updated of every case in his jurisdiction.

Numbers 35:30 points out that more than one witness is required before the penalty of death can be applied. Verses 31 and 32 point out ransom *in lieu* of the prescribed death penalty or exile in a city of refuge is not acceptable. Verse 33 points out the blood of a murder victim pollutes (curses?) the land; this pollution is not removed until the murderer is put to death.

In Deuteronomy 17:6-7, the principle of two or three eye witnesses being necessary for a person to be put to death is reaffirmed, although in this case the offense was the worship of other gods such as the sun or moon.

The 19th Chapter of Deuteronomy sheds light cases involving capital punishment and reaffirms earlier provisions. Verses 2 to 7 reaffirm the concept of cities of refuge where those who accidentally kill another can find refuge. However, Verses 11 and 12 point out the cities of refuge is not for those who hate their neighbor lie in wait and "…smite him mortally that he die…" because the elders of his city can "…send and fetch him thence, and deliver him into the hands of the avenger of blood, that the murderer shall die."

Verse 15 has good advice: "One witness shall not rise up against a man for any iniquity, or for any sin, in any sin that he sinneth: at the mouth of two witnesses or at the mouth of three witnesses shall the matter be established."

Deuteronomy 20:16-21 offers an interesting approach to those who falsely bring legal claims:

"If a false witness rise up against any man to testify against him that which is wrong, then both the men between whom the controversy is, shall stand before the Lord, before thee and the judges, which shall be in those days."

"And the judges shall make diligent inquisition: and behold, if the witness be a false witness and hath testified against his brother;"

"Then shall ye do unto him, as he had thought to have done unto his brother; so shalt thou put the evil way from among you."

"And those which remain shall hear, and fear, and shall henceforth commit no more any such evil among you."

"And thine eye shall not pity; but life shall go for life, eye for eye, tooth for tooth, hand for hand, foot for foot."

Note the deterrent effect claimed. This effect was claimed from the practice of having those who bring false charges suffering the penalty they wished to see applied upon others, including even capital punishment. Again, not feeling sorry for those who are so punished is reaffirmed.

What would be the effect if such a provision were part of the legal structure of the United States? Wouldn't this clear the courts of many nuisance lawsuits?

It is quite clear the Bible does not prohibit the death penalty for murders, but in fact, prescribes a method of swift punishment. Once it had been determined that death was the penalty for a crime word was given to the avenger of blood. From that moment forward the murderer was killed on sight by the avenger of blood. Using an avenger of blood to kill on sight seems a bit harsh, but these scriptures do establish the religious basis for capital punishment.

And what with the forensic science of today, prosecutors, in many cases, can be certain beyond any doubt that it is only the guilty party who is charged with a capital offense. We must be certain, as the death penalty is final, if the death penalty is to be just.

It is no secret there have been staggering numbers of cases where there have been miscarriages of justice. Known murderers have been acquitted. The innocent have been found guilty and even put to death. These miscarriages of justice are more frequent when minorities are involved.

One wonders what would have been the fate in biblical times if the avenger of blood had made a mistake and killed an innocent person. One suspects the penalty for such would involve a second avenger of blood. After all, in biblical times, it was an eye for an eye and tooth for a tooth dating back to the days of Noah. This is to suggest some sort of penalty is needed to counteract cases where the innocent are condemned. And, perhaps even where the guilty are acquitted. Again one wonders what the educative effect would be of such laws in our society.

This call for certainty does not undermine the fact that legally, morally, and religiously, the death penalty has a place in society.

By Richard Salazar Ph.D.

Personal Thoughts

Would Gary Gilmore have had a more acceptable personality if he had been raised in a better childhood environment? Could he have been rehabilitated after his crimes? Such speculation is best left to psychologists. The truth is we will never know a definitive answer to these and many other Gilmore questions. We are left with our own suppositions.

In Gary's case, we see a kid unwanted and abused by his father. His father, Frank, had doubts that Gary was his child, and treated him and the rest of the family with violence. Gary saw that Frank drank heavily and was a con artist. For no apparent reason, Frank often just deserted the family for long periods. Gary began to defy authority, started hanging out with a bad crowd, and there seemed to be no adult available to turn him around. He began swearing, playing around with guns, stealing, smoking, drinking, and skipping school. He started to get a kick out of coming close to suicide, by playing Russian roulette and dodging trains.

Remember, this was an otherwise smart kid, with an IQ of 130; he started to learn that whatever he wanted, he could just take. Not surprisingly, he dropped out of school and began stealing cars. Although he was in and out of prison for many years for theft and assault, it is likely that he received no rehabilitation there. We do know he was beaten by guards, subject to shock therapy, given tranquilizers, put into solitary confinement, and eventually released to a halfway house. Although offered an art scholarship for a local college, he blew it. He was also given a chance to start a new life with relatives; but instead he wanted to continue a life of crime, coming to a stop only when he was served the death penalty for committing two murders. These murders seemed to be precipitated simply by his inability to handle his emotions when his girlfriend tried to break up with him.

It is very difficult to change people after they have become adults or even teenagers. What we become is half due to our inherited personality. The other half of what we call our "own" personality is really influenced by our environment, so that such disparate variables as our own life experiences, along with the behavior patterns shown and taught to us by family, friends, teachers, television, and the like while growing up, are all part of the spice that forms the stew of our own selves.

However, some recent studies (over the past twenty years) show some new schools of thought towards criminal behavior and its causes.

For years, society was accused as the sole culprit; it was thought that society was the reason for criminal behavior. For decades, the convicts were said to have committed crimes because they were victims of poverty, divorce, racism, and a society that denies them opportunities.

Recent studies, though, and Gary's past, show that criminals do know right from wrong, but that they believe that whatever they want to do is right for them. They feel that to commit the crime is justified because they get what they desire (a need for instant gratification). But psychopathic criminals like Gary feel no remorse for those they have hurt. The trauma placed upon the real victim—such as the loss of a loved one, or the loss of property, perhaps the loss of all sanity in the case of rape—all such things are irrelevant to the perpetrator. In the criminal mind, the only thing wrong with committing a crime is getting caught. But if a crime is committed against them, they view that crime as wrong.

The critical factors in becoming a criminal are not race or peer pressure, but rather the character of an individual and the choices he or she makes. There are families in which one child of many chooses to commit crimes, or at least chooses to fulfill the "black sheep" role. The one child grows up to become a criminal, in spite of the fact that all of the rest the children, who were raised in the same environment, do not become criminals.

We must all deal with the circumstances we face. If we want more out of life, we must work harder to acquire those things that we imagine we need and not take what we want from others through violence or other types of crime. We can lower or raise our expectations for what life offers us through control of our attitude towards life.

I have repeatedly dealt with people in trouble, so I know that any teens can end up as criminals. Some youths are raised in well-to-do homes and are given almost anything they desired when they were children. Their parents, rightly or wrongly, considered spoiling their children to be an act of love. The only thing these parents didn't give their kids was much of their time. I'm sure these parents meant well, but often the children they raise suffer later on. When it's time to face life on their own, having to be accountable and responsible for behavior and income, it is difficult to suddenly change a life of learned behavior—instant gratification through whining or otherwise cajoling. So while growing up, money and possessions were given to them freely with little personal effort except maybe the energy expended on manipulating "the folks." Thus many of these kids, in later years, turn to shortcuts such as crime.

The pursuit of wealth often produces what we now call "dual-income families." Both parents working outside the home places the children of such families in the hands of caretakers who cannot love and care for those children as parents should. But in our society, the Smiths must keep up with the Joneses. So kids are increasingly being looked after by teachers, after-school care assistants, librarians, coaches, neighbors, older children, and relatives. What is more important: having a new car, or spending time with your children? Some parents do not give their children sufficient personal time; perhaps they should have considered not having children.

Kids should not see their parents pursuing only personal gratification, wealth, trends, and popularity. Children can be required to work for the things that they want. When they put forth the effort to get what they want, they can find and experience the feeling of self-achievement or self-worth.

From television today, children learn early that the world has a drug problem, wars, a lack of respect for the law, eroding morals and values, and a disregard for other people and the property of others. Today, children spend so much time in front of the television or computer that they're not going out to play games with the kids on the block. And their parents may not be spending much time with them, either.

So the family deteriorates and the unguided young become disaffected. Clearly even kids from "good" homes can become school shooters. Or when they see their parents being violent to each other, they then may grow up also to be violent in relationships.

The Legacy of the Gilmore Gun

In December 2005, media headlines again reminded us of the importance of the Gary Gilmore case as a historical milepost. Headlines appeared such as "The 1,000th Execution since the Death of Gary Gilmore." Gary's execution is now frequently echoed as a permanent anniversary and symbol in these contentious times. In any civilized society, arguments for and against the death penalty will remain, along with other polarizing subjects such as abortion or same-sex marriage, to name some current points of difference.

After more than a decade as a bondsman this is a brief record of the charges for bail bonds. The charges are from most to least frequent:

1. Traffic violations—speeding, no insurance, and so forth
2. Driving under the influence—either alcohol or drugs
3. Driving on a suspended or revoked driver's license
4. Possession of drugs and/or a controlled substance
5. Domestic violence
6. Possession of drug paraphernalia
7. Theft and/or burglary

I have dealt with only three cases dealing with firearm-related charges. There was one charge of a felon possessing a firearm; one charge of theft of a firearm; and one charge of discharging a firearm in the city limits.

Considering the quantity of firearms in my geographic area and the amount of bonds I have written, I don't feel as though my local area, despite Gary's murders, has a serious problem with firearms.

As I was researching the Gilmore Gun's documents, I reviewed the Utah County Attorney's Affidavit which had been typed and notarized on two separate copies. After closer examination, I could see why. There were a dozen typos on the first attempt, including the wrong serial number leaving one digit out. Whoever typed it was struggling that day.

I checked the second affidavit and the serial number was wrong again. I called the original owner, Gordon Swan, and asked if he had ever noticed the error. No one had acknowledged the typo. I contacted the current County Attorney's office and explained to them what I had found and asked if they would help me correct the mistake by issuing another affidavit. The presiding County Attorney refused to help or even talk to me. He told the receptionist to tell me he had nothing to do with it then and wanted nothing to do with it now.

I later contacted Noall Wootton's law office, in American Fork, Utah. He was the Utah County prosecuting attorney of Gilmore's case. I found that Mr. Wootton was very ill making him unable to issue a replacement affidavit and he shortly thereafter passed away.

The affidavit is not that important as far as authenticating the Gilmore Gun, considering the other documentation. Having the FBI lab reports, the pistol, and the Browning manufacturing records certainly documenting there are no flaws in the authenticity of this gun.

I approached the Provo City police department asking if I might review the case records. Police records are not open to the public without permission, unlike court documents. To obtain permission you are required to show identification and sign a request. They said the process would take a few days. The next week, I returned for their response. They denied me access and they asked why I was requesting these records again. I replied I had not previously done so. The office worker said, "Oh yes you have; it was a couple months ago." Again I stated, "I have not requested these records before." Then another woman became involved in the discussion. After further conversation I discovered that someone else had requested the records, claiming to be me, and had said that he was seeking the serial number of the pistol. That's why the police department presumed I had requested the records earlier. I was very concerned that someone was impersonating me and curious as to his desire for records. I asked if I could see the request sheets for the month this had happened, but I was denied again. I wanted to see the request sheets to verify that he had used false identification using my name. The police department's response to me was "Oh, that was a couple of months ago, and we have requests every month." I asked, "How many requests do you normally receive per month?" They replied, "Sometimes only a few, but other times we could get dozens in a month." I offered to read through their excessive paperwork myself, so that they would not have to put any time into the task. They still would not comply and it seemed as if the illicit act of impersonation was of no concern to them. The police did tell me that the records showed that the murder weapon was returned to Gordon Swan. I never doubted that fact but merely wanted more tangible confirmation of other information.

I have spent thousands of hours and dollars researching the Gilmore Gun. In my obsession, I learned more about this tragedy and violent crime than perhaps I care to know. I often wonder, was my acquaintance with the people in this case just coincidence, or maybe meant to be? I retain the hope of turning this rare item and my knowledge about it into something positive, by creating a facility to help those children who need guidance, somewhere to spend productive time and to better educate people about firearms Perhaps helping them make a more rational decision as to whether they prefer to own or not to own firearms.

In any case, by my research, I have become a small part of history, and I have a tangible piece of this rare historical story.

My first book was titled "The Gilmore Gun and I." As soon as the book began to be read by the public numerous other stories began to find me. It seemed as though not a week went by for months without someone approaching or emailing me with another Gilmore experience. I stopped printing after the first run but continued researching and gathering more information. I also read more books on writing technique and attended more classes. I feel this is a much better book than my first attempt.

The interest in the first book was favorable leading to some radio and television talk show interviews. One of my favorite was the radio talk show titled "Live Fire" it is hosted by Larry Pratt who is also the Executive Director of GOA – Gun Owners of America who is a support organization of the second amendment. Live Fire is an hour long radio show and is broadcasted over most of the nation once a week. The show has some very interesting and high profile guests. I have spoken with Larry numerous times since and have found him to be very knowledgeable with a great sense of humor. He is a wonderful speaker and truly cares about our right to bear arms.

I have since been contacted by several movie producers but have only been impressed by one. Toby Dye, producer and director, contacted me from England saying he was interested in my story. After a telephone conversation I agreed to send him both of my books while he agreed to send me two of his latest documentary movies. I have long enjoyed documentaries and was very pleased with his work. He also stated he felt the same of mine. At this time we are still negotiating.

During the past seven years of researching, brokering, buying, selling this gun, I have had more bizarre offers of all kinds than I care to tell. Everything from money, cars, land, favors of all kinds, and promises you can only imagine.

The Gilmore Gun was placed on an auction July of 2008 with a beginning bid of only ninety nine cents. The auction lasted two months receiving almost five thousand bids reaching one million dollars but still did not reach the reserve price. It did not sell.

Can an object such as this pistol contain some kind of "memory" or evil presence? Could it possess a negative or positive energy that could influence someone, or be felt in any way? Some think so. People have held this gun and swear that they sense an uncomfortable feeling. Others have said it gives them sensations such as chills or confusion. Some have refused to even touch it. Others swear it is a cursed item. Perhaps it is just the thought of what mayhem someone caused with this piece of wood and steel. Conceivably it is possible to turn this tragedy into some level of triumph.

I believe some people are evil, not objects. One thing I do know: the Gilmore Gun is one of a kind.

Bibliography

Sources: Bureau of Justice Statistics, Capital Punishment 2003 report; Federal Death Penalty Resource Counsel Project.

Sources for section about Utah:
1. Gillespie, L. Kay. (1994). "Capital Punishment in Utah," p.73 in Utah History Encyclopedia, edited by Allan Kent Powell. Salt Lake City, Utah: University of Utah Press.
2. U.S. Department of Health & Human Services.

Sources for Chapter 9:
Amnesty International. (1999). "List of Abolitionist and Retentionist Countries." Report ACT 50/01/99, April, 1999. Retrieved from Amnesty International. (1999). "List of Abolitionist and Retentionist Countries." Report ACT 50/01/99, April, 1999.Retrieved from http://www.web.amnesty.orgai.nsf/index/ACT500052000

Baker, D. (1999). "A Descriptive Profile and Socio-Historical Analysis of Female Executions in the United States: 1632–1997." Women and Criminal Justice, 10(3), 57.

Bedau, H. (ed.) (1997). The Death Penalty in America: Current Controversies. New York: Oxford University Press.

Bohm, R. 1999. Deathquest: An Introduction to the Theory and Practice of Capital Punishment in the United States. Cincinnati: Anderson Publishing.

Death Penalty Information Center. Accessible at http://www.deathpenaltyinfo.org/ .
Michigan State University and Death Penalty Information Center. (2000). "History of the Death Penalty." Retrieved from http://deathpenaltyinfo.msu.edu/
O'Shea, K. (1999). Women and the Death Penalty in the United States, 1900–1998. Westport, CT: Praeger.
Randa, L. (ed.) (1997). Society's Final Solution: A History and Discussion of the Death Penalty. Lanham, MD: University Press of America, 1997.
Schabas, W. (1999). The Abolition of the Death Penalty in International Law (2nd ed.). New York: Cambridge University Press.
Streib, V. (June, 2003). Death Penalty for Female Offenders, January 1973 to June 2003. Ada, OH: Ohio Northern University. Available online.
U.S. Department of Justice, Bureau of Justice Statistics. (November, 2004). Capital Punishment Annual. National Criminal Justice (NCJ) 206627.
U.S. Department of Justice, Bureau of Justice Statistics correctional surveys. (The National Probation Survey, National Prisoner Statistics, Survey of Jails, and The National Parole Survey).

Acknowledgements

Thank you to all who helped with documentation and personal experiences. A special thanks to Larry Boltz for his help in writing, editing, encouragement and belief in me.

About the Author

A native of Spanish Fork, Utah, Dennis R. Stilson is personally acquainted with many of the people touched by the crimes of Gary Gilmore. As one of the owners through the experiences of the Gilmore Gun, he's uniquely qualified to tell its tale and offer an examination of the criminal, the crime, and the use of the ultimate penalty.

Dennis's childhood was not uneventful. At ten years of age, Dennis avoided being hit by a train by only inches, having been thrown from a startled horse. He did survive, however, growing up with two sisters but losing a brother at 3 years of age. He began boxing at age ten and remained very active for a decade. As a teen, Dennis worked as a paperboy and lifeguard.

This man in boots has seen a lot of life. He has saved two people from drowning. For a time, he worked for Robert Redford in the stables at the Sundance Ski Resort. He trained as a pilot, managed a furniture store, toured the west as a singer and guitarist, sold solar and water equipment, ran cable for TV, striped highways, and sold golfing gear and cars. He was a fishing guide in Alaska, a financial advisor, and was in advertising. Finally he was a pawnbroker, gun show dealer, bail bondsman, and single parent.

He is currently a Utah State hunter safety instructor and shooting range safety officer.

Dennis's life has revolved around the "G" words: God, guns, guitars, girls, and golf. The order of the last four may vary, depending on the weather. Firearms have always been part of Dennis's life. The past years of dealing with the Gilmore Gun and finding out more its story have changed his life. He hopes one day to build and operate a positive facility to help educate others concerning patriotism and firearms for a better understanding which will hopefully lead to better decisions. He has now formed a non profit organization called Guns for Good Inc.